from the author of TEEN PEOPLE OF THE BIBLE

CRASH COURSE

forming a faith foundation for life

DANIEL DARLING

NEW HOPE
PUBLISHERS

Birmingham, Alabama

New Hope® Publishers
P. O. Box 12065
Birmingham, AL 35202–2065
www.newhopepublishers.com
New Hope Publishers is a division of WMU®

Library of Congress Cataloging-in-Publication Data

Darling, Daniel, 1978-
  Crash course : forming a faith foundation for life / Daniel Darling.
    p. cm.
  ISBN 978-1-59669-285-5 (sc)
  1. Spiritual formation. I. Title.
  BV4501.3.D373 2010
  248.4--dc22
                          2010001761

Cover design by Arthur Cherry, arthuradesign.com
Interior design by Kathy Sealy

ISBN-10: 1-59669-285-5
ISBN-13: 978-1-59669-285-5

N114130 • 0410 • 3M1

DEDICATION

To Ben Kottwitz, devoted husband, loving father, man of God. I was fortunate to call Ben my friend. Ben, your life on earth was short, but your impact was great. I pray I live with the same consistency, integrity, and passion.

CONTENTS

ACKNOWLEDGMENTS 8

INTRODUCTION 10

⊕ SECTION ONE

DOCTRINE—KNOWING WHAT YOU BELIEVE AND WHY 13

Day 1 14
Day 2 16
Day 3 18
Day 4 20
Day 5 22
Day 6 24
Day 7 26
Day 8 28
Day 9 30
Day 10 32
Day 11 34
Day 12 36
Day 13 38
Day 14 40
Day 15 42
Day 16 44
Day 17 46
Day 18 48
Day 19 50
Day 20 52

SECTION ONE RESOURCES 54

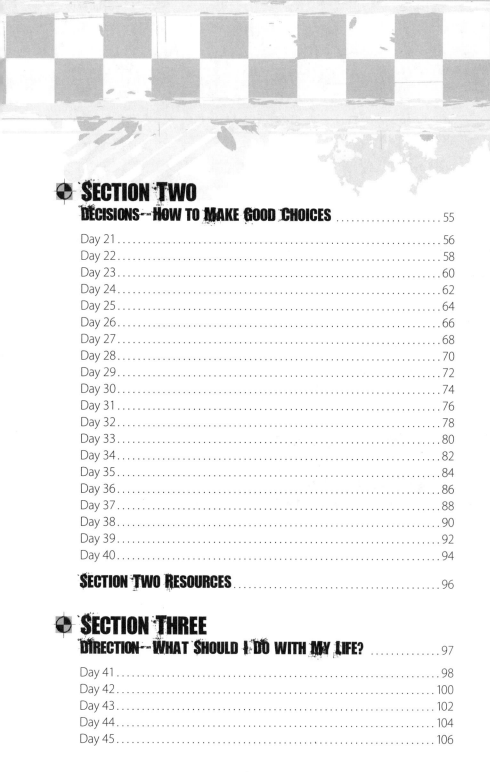

⊕ SECTION TWO
DECISIONS--HOW TO MAKE GOOD CHOICES 55

Day 21 56
Day 22 58
Day 23 60
Day 24 62
Day 25 64
Day 26 66
Day 27 68
Day 28 70
Day 29 72
Day 30 74
Day 31 76
Day 32 78
Day 33 80
Day 34 82
Day 35 84
Day 36 86
Day 37 88
Day 38 90
Day 39 92
Day 40 94

SECTION TWO RESOURCES 96

⊕ SECTION THREE
DIRECTION--WHAT SHOULD I DO WITH MY LIFE? 97

Day 41 98
Day 42 100
Day 43 102
Day 44 104
Day 45 106

Day 46 108
Day 47 110
Day 48 112
Day 49 114
Day 50 116
Day 51 118
Day 52 120
Day 53 122
Day 54 124
Day 55 126
Day 56 128
Day 57 130
Day 58 132
Day 59 134
Day 60 136

SECTION THREE RESOURCES 138

⊕ SECTION FOUR
DEVOTION--STAYING TRUE IN A WORLD OF LIES 139

Day 61 140
Day 62 142
Day 63 144
Day 64 146
Day 65 148
Day 66 150
Day 67 152
Day 68 154
Day 69 156
Day 70 158
Day 71 160
Day 72 162
Day 73 164
Day 74 166

Day 75 168
Day 76 170
Day 77 172
Day 78 174
Day 79 176
Day 80 178

SECTION FOUR RESOURCES 180

⊕ SECTION FIVE
DELIGHT—FINDING JOY IN A HARD WORLD 181

Day 81 182
Day 82 184
Day 83 186
Day 84 188
Day 85 190
Day 86 192
Day 87 194
Day 88 196
Day 89 198
Day 90 200
Day 91 202
Day 92 204
Day 93 206
Day 94 208
Day 95 210
Day 96 212
Day 97 214
Day 98 216
Day 99 218
Day 100 220

SECTION FIVE RESOURCES 222

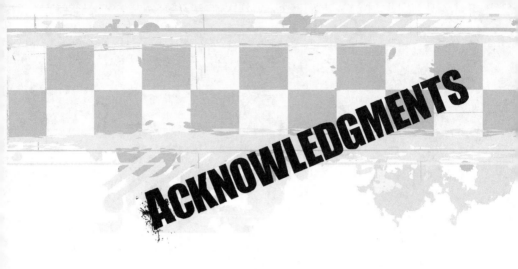

ACKNOWLEDGMENTS

A book is never the work of one; it's a collaborative effort. I would call these people a team but that would be so perfectly cliché, like I ripped it from a leadership conference. I enjoy conferences, hate clichés, but here it goes.

Most authors praise their wives last, but I can't get away with that, because it has always been Angela who has nurtured my dreams. Whenever God sparks a book idea in my head and heart, she says, "Go for it." When others have doubted, she has believed. Plus, she allows me to spend quality time with my laptop while she manages the "mini-zoo" that is our family. Of the good choices I've made, marrying Angela was the best. She is a godly woman with a passion for seeing people's lives enriched by connection to God and His Word.

I'm deeply grateful to Andrea Mullins, publisher extraordinaire at New Hope. She first believed in me, an unproven writer with a slim string of published articles, some crazy ideas, and a lot of purple prose. Andrea has a love for God and a love for people unparalleled by anyone in this industry. It's a high honor to count her as one of my friends.

I'm also indebted to the rest of the team at New Hope. Jonathan Howe, marketing manager, whose driving in Dallas made me carsick, but whose energy, passion, and love for theology make us kindred spirits. Joyce Dinkins is a professional's professional, whose demand for excellence sharpens me as an author. And nobody prays quite like Joyce. The rest of the co-laborers are top-notch: editor Randy Bishop, copy editor Kathryne Solomon, and publicity specialist Ashley Stephens.

Les Stobbe lent great wisdom in shaping this book and working as my agent with New Hope. Les is a giant in the publishing industry and has a legacy of connecting gifted biblical communicators with the readers who need to hear the Word.

I'm grateful to the many friends who volunteered to read through the manuscript—especially those horrid first drafts: Julie Dearyan, Suzanne Slade, Dawn Hill, Sherri Gallagher, Kris Long, Eddie Schultz, and Donna Clark Goodrich.

Two pastors looked through with a theological eye: Pastor Bill Swanger, a mentor and friend; and Pastor Dave Ralph, my good friend, who also gave me the unvarnished advice I sought.

Tim Darling, who is not only my brother in the Lord, but is also my actual brother, gave terrific ideas. His passion for God and for youth is contagious. The fact that we get to do ministry together is one of God's richest blessings to me.

Joanna Davidson is the talented editor who helped make my writing look good. She's a gifted writer, editor, and friend. Her attention to detail is extraordinary.

Lastly, I must thank God the Father, whose gift of the Holy Spirit has enabled me to communicate the message. Henry Blackaby is known to have said that God purposely calls us to tasks much larger than ourselves so that we're forced to depend on Him. This book is a work much too big for me; it's only by God's sovereign grace that it happened.

STANDIN' ON THE ROCK

When Christmas break rolls around, some travel to vacation spots. Others hang out at home and play video games. Some go to camps or concerts.

Not me when I was younger. I got up before the sun, threw on five layers, and shuffled off to a construction site.

Cold, dark, and five hours too early.

My dad is a contractor. One of those guys who can build anything. But for some reason that fix-it gene skipped a generation.

Give me a pair of wrenches or a hammer and I'm lost. Plop me in front of a computer and I'm golden.

So those cold, tired days in construction didn't turn me into an extreme makeover star, but they did teach me a few important lessons.

Don't cut a live wire.

Don't hit your thumb with a hammer.

Make sure every house has a good foundation.

That last one really stuck. I'll never forget a story about some builders who thought they could save cash by cheating on the foundation. Bad idea.

A few Chicago winters caused the foundation to settle and the walls to slip. The owners weren't happy. Apparently, people don't like huge cracks in their living room walls. Who knew?

The penny-pinching wise guys had to come back and start over again.

Jesus said something about foundations (Matthew 7:24–27). Every life, He said, is like a house. It should be built on something rock-solid.

ROCK PAPER SAND

Right now, you're in the foundation-building place in your life. The decisions you make, the patterns you form, and the beliefs you adopt form the foundation that determines your future.

So where do we find the firm stuff we need for a solid foundation? The Bible says there is only one sure foundation—Jesus Christ (1 Corinthians 3:11).

You say:

"I've got Jesus. I'm religious. I believe." Or,

"My parents are Christians so I must be a Christian." Or,

"I do youth group every week—though I sleep through church every Sunday—and I even sing on the worship team."

You may think that's all good, but is your life truly built on the Rock? Do you *know* what you believe?

Not what your youth pastor believes.

Not what your mamma believes.

Not what your Bible-smart goody-two-shoes friend believes.

Here's the deal. You're about to walk out of the comfort zone and into real life. Are you ready?

I don't want to scare you, but this isn't high school anymore. And if you don't know *exactly* what you believe, you'll get tossed around like a tent in a tornado.

So, for the next 100 days, we're going to discuss just what it means to be a follower of Christ. We're going to take a *Crash Course* in five critical areas:

- **Doctrine**—*Knowing What You Believe and Why*
- **Decisions**—*How to Make Good Choices*
- **Direction**—*What Should I Do with My Life?*
- **Devotion**—*Staying True in a World of Lies*
- **Delight**—*Finding Joy in a Hard World*

Do me a favor. Take the next 100 days and get serious about building that foundation. Read through each devotional. Reflect on the Bible verses. But don't just take my word for it. Investigate each idea and make it your own. Discuss these devotions with your pastor, your friends, your family.

Then pray and ask God to help you formulate a game plan for life.

SECTION ONE

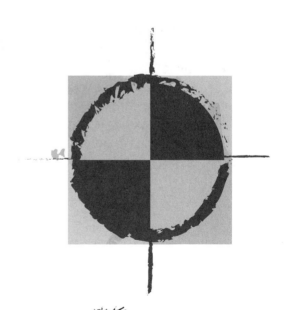

DOCTRINE—
KNOWING WHAT YOU BELIEVE AND WHY

DAY 1

THE TRUTH MAP

A few years ago, Angela and I were visiting South Bend, Indiana. As a football fan, I wanted to see the Notre Dame Hall of Fame, where the legend of Knute Rockne lives. We parked at the university's information office and grabbed a campus map. It's not a very big campus, but big enough for us to lose our way. Instead of ending up at the football stadium, we arrived at the performing arts center.

The problem wasn't the map. The problem was the person holding the map. There was only one way to the football stadium, and we didn't take it.

The Bible is the map for life. It says that Jesus is the only way to reach God. But people often want to say, "That's your version of truth. I've got mine."

Well, you might have your beliefs and I might have mine, but there can only be one right way.

Imagine if I took that Notre Dame campus map and tossed it aside in favor of a map more to my liking. I might discover a lot of cool buildings, but probably wouldn't see the inside of the stadium.

That's what happens to those who reject the truth. They're headed for a life of confusion and may never end up where they were intended to be: safe in the arms of God.

Why is **one truth** better than any **other** truth?

BOTTOM LINE

Truth is a matter of life and death. If Jesus Christ is the only way, then all other ways to God are false in their basis—and are paths to destruction.

OWN IT

For a good comparison of world religions, check out *They Can't All Be Right: Do All Spiritual Paths Lead to God?* by Steve Russo.

POWER PRAYER: *Dear God, I don't want to live a life of confusion. Help me to discover the truth as only You can reveal it.*

POWER PASSAGE

Jesus said to him,

"I am the way,

and the truth,

and the life.

No one comes

to the Father

except through me."

John 14:6

DAY 2

WHAT'S THE BIG DEAL ABOUT THE BOOK?

What do you think is the best-selling book of all time? *Harry Potter*? *Left Behind*? Would you be shocked to learn that it's the Bible? Some say 2.5 billion copies have been sold. Others say it is closer to 6 billion.

If you live in America, it's hard to escape the Bible. You can buy one at any drug store. You can read it online in almost every language. You can download it onto your phone. The Bible is everywhere.

So what's the big deal about the Bible anyway? Is it just another book?

Not only is the Bible the most historically accurate document in the history of the world, but the Bible is the living, breathing Word of God. In 2 Timothy, it says the Bible was actually *"breathed out by God."*

You say, "How do we know that this wasn't just a bunch of people long ago who put together a nice book and claimed it was from God?" We know that because it would have been impossible for 40 different writers, who lived across more than a thousand years, to create a book that has the same story line throughout its pages.

The books, the letters, the poems, the stories, the prophecies that make up the Scriptures were all inspired by God. They are God's words. And God used humans to write them. First Peter says that *"holy men of God spoke as they were moved by the Holy Spirit"* (2 Peter 1:21 NKJV).

I dare you. Crack open this best-selling book today. And when you do, remember that you're not reading just any other book, you're listening to the voice of God (Romans 3:2).

Is the **Bible** just **another book** or is there **something more** to it?

BOTTOM LINE

The Bible is God's love letter. Everything God wants us to know for now, He put in there.

OWN IT

If you want more proof about the accuracy of the Bible, go to gotquestions.org and under the "Crucial Questions" tab, click on "Is the Bible Truly God's Word?"

POWER PRAYER: *Dear God, thank You for giving us Your complete, written Word. I know it is You speaking to me. I want to treasure Your words and sew them into the fabric of my heart.*

POWER PASSAGE

All Scripture is breathed out by God and profitable for teaching, for reproof, for correction, and for training in righteousness, that the man of God may be competent, equipped for every good work.

2 Timothy 3:16–17

HOW DID WE GET HERE IN THE FIRST PLACE?

When I was 12, I dissected our family's toaster and then tried to put it back together. After 5 hours and 15 extra parts, I plugged it in. The little appliance gave off a weird smell. Black smoke curled out of the inside, setting off our smoke alarm. My career as an engineer was over before it began.

Putting a toaster together is a pretty simple operation if you're not mechanically challenged like me. But imagine if I'd just taken the parts, thrown them in a shoebox, and vigorously shaken it. How long would I have to shake the box before the parts formed into a working toaster? An hour? A day? A week?

Obviously, you could shake that box forever and it still wouldn't produce a working toaster. Somebody has to put the parts together.

What about the parts of the human body? Who put those together? Some say we just kind of happened here by chance. That over millions of years, millions of little cells just magically formed into the complexity of Creation.

The Bible says we got here in a much more dignified way (Genesis 1; John). In Genesis we read that the world was created by God, the Master Designer, Artist, and Craftsman. By the word of His mouth, everything came into existence. His hands (so to speak) sculpted humankind from the dust of the ground.

I may not be smart enough to assemble a toaster, but I'm also not dumb enough to believe we got here merely by chance.

Did humans **evolve slowly** over time or did a **Designer** create us with a purpose?

BOTTOM LINE

If evolution is true, then life has no purpose. If the Creation story in Genesis is true, then God has a unique purpose for every person.

OWN IT

Work with your parents or youth pastor to organize a trip to the Creation Museum in Kentucky (creationmuseum.org). Or rent the movie *Expelled* by Ben Stein.

POWER PRAYER: *Dear God, I'm glad I'm not here by chance, but by design. Thank You for Your creativity and purpose in creating this beautiful world.*

WHO IS GOD?

E ven if you snoozed through science class, you know that water has three forms: ice, liquid, and vapor. Each element is water, yet each has a distinct form and purpose.

If you think that's interesting, here's an idea that will blow you away. The Bible says God has three forms called the "Trinity." God the Father, Jesus Christ the Son, and the Holy Spirit. All three are distinct persons and yet the three are all equally only one God.

The Son's death on the Cross gives us access to the Father. The Spirit's empowering presence helps us bring glory to God.

Theologians, pastors, and authors have written volumes on this subject, yet no human has ever grasped its depth. But our inability to understand the magnitude of God doesn't make the doctrine of the Trinity less true. The truth of the Trinity is an essential part of our Christian faith.

The Trinity is also an essential part of your spiritual walk. Because of the work of the Son, you can know the Father who loves you. And because of the Holy Spirit inside of you, your life can bring glory to the Father.

It is more complicated than liquid, ice, and vapor, but it's also infinitely more valuable.

How can **God** be **one God** and yet be in **three distinct forms**?

BOTTOM LINE

Many religions try to worship God the Father, but they bypass Jesus Christ, who is God the Son. The Trinity is essential to the Christian faith. Either you accept God for who He is or you don't accept Him at all.

OWN IT

Study these verses, which shed more light on the nature of the Trinity: Matthew 28:19; 2 Corinthians 13:13–14; 1 John 2:22–23; Revelation 1:4–6.

POWER PRAYER: *Dear God, I don't really understand how You can be one and yet three. Honestly, it seems kind of complicated. But I'm grateful that You care enough to be my God and my Savior and to give me strength each day through Your Spirit.*

POWER PASSAGE

Then God said, "Let us make man in our image, after our likeness. And let them have dominion over the fish of the sea and over the birds of the heavens and over the livestock and over all the earth and over every creeping thing that creeps on the earth."

Genesis 1:26

DAY 5

WHO IS JESUS?

I'm not exactly sure how you came to read this book. Maybe you were bored and had nothing else to do. Maybe your parents made you read it. Maybe a friend threw it in your locker. I don't know.

But perhaps you're curious. Curious about one question: *Who exactly is Jesus?* There are lots of opinions. Some think Jesus was just a good teacher. Some think He was a religious figure. Some think He was a revolutionary political leader.

I think the best way to find out who He was is to listen to what He said. And if you listen closely by reading the Gospels (Matthew, Mark, Luke, and John), you'll quickly discover that Jesus claimed to be something much more than just a good teacher or religious leader. Jesus claimed to be God, sent from Heaven.

His claim is bulletproof. He was born of Mary, who was a virgin. He lived a sinless life. He performed supernatural miracles. He fulfilled every prophecy. That's why the people of His day wanted to put Jesus to death. He claimed to be God in the flesh.

The Bible says that Jesus always is and always was. John 1 and Colossians 1 claim that Jesus was not only present at Creation—He actually *is* the Creator.

Jesus came so we could know God. Therefore, real life rises and falls based on what you do with Jesus. When you embrace Him as your Savior, He is life.

Was **Jesus** just a really **nice guy** or was He **God**?

BOTTOM LINE

If Jesus is one of several ways to God, then Christianity is just another religion. If Jesus is the *only* way to God, then every person needs to know Him.

OWN IT

Watch *The Gospel of John* movie featuring Christopher Plummer. This movie is a vivid narration of the most important book about Jesus.

POWER PRAYER: *Dear Jesus, I know that You are the only way to God, that You are God in the flesh. Help me to live each day for You.*

POWER PASSAGE

He is the radiance of the glory of God and the exact imprint of his nature, and he upholds the universe by the word of his power. After making purification for sins, he sat down at the right hand of the Majesty on high.

Hebrews 1:3–4

BAD ALMOST FROM THE BEGINNING

One of my favorite athletes recently got caught up in a huge scandal. I was disappointed because I thought he was better than that. But what really upset me was that instead of apologizing, he released a really lame statement that basically said, "Hey, nobody's perfect, man."

The athlete is a knucklehead, but in his denial, he stumbled upon something that is actually true.

The Bible does say that nobody's perfect. We read in Romans 3:23 that all have sinned and *"fall short"* of God's glory. If you've taken a breath on planet Earth, you've joined an illustrious club. You're a sinner.

Our sin story began on a terrible day in a beautiful garden. Eve, the very first woman, ignored God's command and ate from the forbidden tree. Then Adam took a bite and the world was changed forever.

Sin and evil and death weren't God's original plan. He created a beautiful world, free of all that is bad. But He also gave us a choice. We chose sin over perfection.

Adam's choice, however, didn't take God by surprise. He already had a solution. That solution is the Savior, promised by God and fulfilled in Jesus Christ.

So it's true, you're not perfect. I'm not perfect. Nobody's perfect. But that's not an impossible barrier, because Jesus is perfect and He offers you new life in Him.

It wasn't **just a piece of fruit** they ate. When our great, great (plus several thousand greats) grandparents ate the **forbidden fruit**, they brought something new and destructive into the world: **sin.**

Therefore, just as sin came into the world through one man, and death through sin, and so death spread to all men because all sinned.

Romans 5:12

BOTTOM LINE

If everyone is a sinner, then everyone needs a Savior. Only one Savior qualifies—Jesus Christ.

OWN IT

Read Adam and Eve's story in Genesis 2–3. Ask yourself these questions: *Would I have eaten that apple? What choices do I make that are sins against God? Why do I tend to choose sin over obedience to God?*

POWER PRAYER: *Dear God, I know that I'm a sinner, that every day I make choices that violate Your holiness. Thank You for providing a solution in Jesus Christ.*

DEAD MEN WALKING

I magine walking into a funeral home and asking a dead man to cook your breakfast or change the oil in your car. If you pulled a stunt like that, someone would come get you and put you in a house with padded walls.

As crazy as it sounds, that's what it's like when people who don't know Jesus Christ try to live a good life. They're like dead men walking. They may *seem* as alive as you and me, but according to God, anyone without the Savior—in an important way—is dead.

And they can do nothing to make themselves alive. No good works. No religious code. Something supernatural must happen.

Jesus says anyone who is dead in sin has to be "made alive" or *"born again"* (John 3:3). Thankfully, Jesus did the hard part. When He died on the Cross and rose again, He defeated sin and death. The easy part—accepting the free offer of salvation—is up to us.

When you put your faith in Christ, something happens inside of you. Your spirit is born again. You're not dead anymore. You're alive.

How many
good works
does it take
to **get to heaven?**

BOTTOM LINE

Jesus said that to enter the kingdom of heaven, you must be born again. (John 3:3)

OWN IT

Read Jesus's dialogue with Nicodemus in John 3:1–15. Then read Ephesians 2:1–10. Ask yourself, *Just how many good works would it take for me to get to Heaven?*

POWER PRAYER: *Dear God, I know I don't deserve your mercy. Thank You for being the bridge between my sin and a holy God. I'm in awe of Your grace. I bow down and worship You.*

POWER PASSAGE

And you were dead in the trespasses and sins in which you once walked, following the course of this world, following the prince of the power of the air, the spirit that is now at work in the sons of disobedience— among whom we all once lived in the passions of our flesh, carrying out the desires of the body and the mind, and were by nature children of wrath, like the rest of mankind.

Ephesians 2:1–3

DAY 8

WHY TRYING HARDER WON'T WORK

When I got out of high school, I had the bright idea of learning to Rollerblade™. Now if you know me, you know I'm about as coordinated as a giraffe on a skateboard. So I bought some Rollerblades™ and set off for the biggest hill I could find.

The downhill part was cool—all 4.5 seconds of it. But when I ended up in a heap at the bottom of the hill, I realized two things: (1) Pavement really hurts, and (2) As hard as I tried, it just wasn't in me to Rollerblade™.

I packed up the blades and sold them on E-bay.

A lot of religious people think if they work really hard, they can get to heaven. They think that if they pull a Mother Teresa, God will overlook all of their sins.

There's a problem with that. Everybody has a different standard of what's right and what's wrong. So who's to say how many good works are enough?

Actually, you'd have to be perfect your entire life. That's the unreachable standard. The Bible says that our attempts to make God happy with our good works are like *"filthy rags"* (Isaiah 64:6 NLT). That doesn't mean we should stop doing good things. It means what we try to do falls way short compared to what God expects.

Here's the deal. Becoming a Christian is not about trying harder. It's not about digging in and doing better. It's about realizing how sinful we are and how holy God is. It's about calling out to God and accepting His gracious gift of forgiveness.

What does **God think** of our **good works**?

BOTTOM LINE

If you try to work your way to heaven, you won't end up there. If you accept Jesus as your Savior, you'll get there.

OWN IT

If you're interested in exploring this idea further, you might check out *How Good Is Good Enough?* by Andy Stanley.

POWER PRAYER: *Dear God, I know I couldn't possibly do enough good works to please You. Thank You for loving me in spite of my sin. I accept Your forgiveness and grace.*

POWER PASSAGE

He saved us,

not because of

works done by us

in righteousness,

but according to

his own mercy,

by the washing

of regeneration

and renewal of

the Holy Spirit.

Titus 3:5

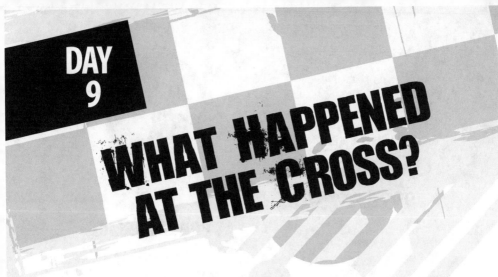

DAY 9
WHAT HAPPENED AT THE CROSS?

I remember the first time I saw *The Passion of the Christ*. I didn't speak during the entire movie. I cried like a baby. Why? Because what happened on that lonely hill of Golgotha 2,000 years ago was more than just a sad story.

You see, Jesus Christ shouldn't have hung there, naked, beaten beyond recognition. Jesus Christ was perfect. He never sinned, not even once.

I should have hung there instead of Him because of my great sin. But God loved me and God loved you so much that He sent Jesus Christ, who is both God and man, to this earth to pay for the sins we commit.

What happened on that Cross? It wasn't just another Roman execution. It was Jesus, the Son of God, taking the punishment for all the sins of the world.

Sin left us separated from God. It destroyed what God once created. But Jesus Christ took your sin and my sin and by His death, gave you and me life. Eternal life.

I've stood at the place where many people believe that Jesus died. I've looked up at the ugly hill shaped like a skull. I know that what happened there happened for me. Because of Jesus's death, God no longer sees my sins. He sees the righteousness of Jesus Christ.

Maybe you think only so-called good, religious people get close to God. Maybe you think He washed His hands of ordinary, messed-up people like you and me.

Do you want to know the truth? God loves everyone, especially those who have messed up in life. Go to the Cross and there

The **death**
of **one Man**
brought **life**
to **everyone**
who believes.

you'll find the same forgiveness and acceptance that I found.

BOTTOM LINE

Because Jesus died, we can have our sins forgiven and our futures eternally changed.

OWN IT

If you want to get a glimpse of the horror of the crucifixion, check out the movie, *The Passion of the Christ*. As you watch, remember that everything Jesus suffered, He suffered for you.

POWER PRAYER: *Dear Jesus, thank You for taking my sin and paying the ultimate price for my freedom and forgiveness.*

POWER PASSAGE

For our sake

he made him

to be sin

who knew no sin,

so that in him

we might become

the righteousness

of God.

2 Corinthians 5:21

DAY 10
AN EMPTY FEELING

I once served as a juror in the trial of a man involved in a violent crime. For an entire week, I sat with 11 other people and listened to the prosecutor and defense attorney each present their side of the case.

The strongest piece of evidence was a witness who claimed to have seen the crime take place. It sealed the deal with us, the jury.

Imagine if there were 500 witnesses. There would be no questions. We wouldn't have had to meet in that hot room for five hours. The prosecutor would have done cartwheels in the courtroom.

Did you know that 500 witnesses saw Jesus after He died? Five hundred people knew He rose from the grave. This is one huge piece of evidence that tells us the Easter story is not just a nice story; it's an historical fact.

But for you and me it's not just history. It's life. Because Jesus rose from the dead, believers in Christ will also rise and live with Him forever.

Did **Jesus** Christ really
rise from the dead
or is that
just a **myth?**

BOTTOM LINE

It's important if Jesus Christ didn't rise from the dead; then He wasn't God; He was an imposter. That would make Christians pretty miserable people, wouldn't it?

OWN IT

Read 1 Corinthians 15:1–19. Ask yourself a few questions: *What are the most powerful evidences of Christ's resurrection? Why is Jesus's resurrection so central to our faith? What does it mean for me personally?*

POWER PRAYER: *Dear Jesus, I believe the resurrection story, and I'm in awe of your power to rise from the dead and give me new life. I want to live my life yielded to You, so that others experience Your life-changing power.*

POWER PASSAGE

For I delivered to you as of first importance what I also received: that Christ died for our sins in accordance with the Scriptures, that he was buried, that he was raised on the third day in accordance with the Scriptures, and that he appeared to Cephas, then to the twelve. Then he appeared to more than five hundred brothers at one time, most of whom are still alive, though some have fallen asleep.

1 Corinthians 15:3–6

PLAYING FOR KEEPS

Have you ever been kicked off a team or kicked out of a school? You felt rejected and alone, didn't you?

Well, there are a lot of people who are afraid of being kicked off God's team. Someone somewhere told them that if they mess up too badly, they'd lose their salvation.

If this is you, I've got great news. The Bible says that once you put your faith in Christ, you have eternal life, and you have it forever. Not temporarily. Not for five years. Not until God finds out all your secrets.

The Bible says that every believer is a child of God (1 John 3:1–2). The Bible also says that every believer has the Holy Spirit inside of him or her until that person gets to heaven (Ephesians 4:30).

Being God's child. Jesus in you. These are forever things, not temporary things.

God loves us. He treasures us. And God doesn't lose the things He treasures. Jesus said that those who believe will *never* perish and that *nobody* (not even yourself) can pluck you out of God's hand. Romans 8:38–39 says that nothing can separate us from God's love. Not a bad day. Not a really big sin. Not even the enemy, Satan.

Doesn't that automatically make your day better? No matter what happens, if you're a child of God, you're secure in His love. He won't lose you.

How many **mistakes** does it take to get **kicked out** of God's family?

BOTTOM LINE

If you've put your trust in Jesus Christ as your Savior, you're a child of God forever. Since God can save you, God will keep you and won't lose you.

OWN IT

Check out these great Bible verses: Romans 8:38–39; 1 John 5:13; John 6:37

POWER PRAYER: *Dear God, thank You, not only for saving me, but also for keeping me. I'm glad I'm Your child forever and that I can never, ever lose my salvation.*

POWER PASSAGE

"I give them eternal life, and they will never perish, and no one will snatch them out of my hand. My Father, who has given them to me, is greater than all, and no one is able to snatch them out of the Father's hand. I and the Father are one."

John 10:28–30

DAY 12

GOD IN YOU

It seems everyone today is talking about spirits and ghosts and forces. This talk is all over the Internet and in movies and music. Most of this stuff is crazy, I think.

The Bible does speak of a Spirit living inside of every believer. But this isn't something weird. It's something wonderful. In fact, the Spirit Who lives in us is the Holy Spirit, who is God—also a third member of the Trinity.

Before Jesus Christ died, the Holy Spirit visited believers, but only as God directed. But when Jesus came, He promised to send a Comforter, the Holy Spirit, to indwell believers after He left (John 14:26).

The Holy Spirit has one important job—to help each of us live the way God wants us to live. Isn't that awesome? He's our greatest helper, teacher, and friend.

You see, God didn't intend for us to try to live this life alone. We're not strong enough. But the Holy Spirit, who is God, is here to steer us away from bad choices, to remind us of God's goodness, and to give us the strength to live a radical life of faith.

Isn't that so much greater than some weird "force"?

What does it mean to have **God dwelling inside** of you?

BOTTOM LINE

If you are a true Christian, you have God inside of you, in the form of the Holy Spirit.

OWN IT

Read these great passages about the Holy Spirit: John 14:26; Galatians 5:22–23. Write down some of the characteristics of the Holy Spirit and what He wants to do in your life.

POWER PRAYER: *Dear Lord, I want to yield control of my life to Your Holy Spirit. Guide me, lead me, and empower me to glorify the Father.*

POWER PASSAGE

Do you not know

that you are

God's temple

and that

God's Spirit

dwells in you?

1 Corinthians 3:16

Teach you all things

He is all knowing and all powerful

Through christ you can keep yourself strong from sin & always experiencing joy

DAY 13

ARE YOU READY?

U nless you're a funeral director, you don't get up in the morning and say, "Hey, let's talk about death." But it's a pretty important subject.

What do you think happens after you die? Here's where we have to rely on what the Bible says.

Hebrews 9:27 says you only die once. So this idea of coming back as a grasshopper or a movie star is just someone's far-out idea.

Then, Jesus said that when we die, we'll go to one of two places (John 5:24–30). We'll either go to heaven, or we'll go to hell. And where we go depends on a very simple choice we make before we die. Those who believe in Jesus Christ will enjoy the pleasures of heaven, and those who reject Jesus suffer the horrors of hell.

Sounds harsh. Can't a loving God make a few exceptions? Actually, God *did* make an exception—for anyone who believes in Jesus Christ, His Son. But most people reject that message (Matthew 7:13–14). They think they've got life and death covered by their good works.

But you don't have to be one of those eternal casualties. And you don't have to let your friends make that fatal mistake either. Share with them the exciting, wonderful news of God's love so you can see them in heaven—forever.

Then death won't be such a scary subject after all.

If you're **ready to die**, then you're **ready to live**. Because if you know Christ, **dying** is just the **beginning of life** the way it was meant to be lived.

BOTTOM LINE

Where you end up after you die depends on the choices you make before you die.

OWN IT

For a great presentation of the gospel message, go to YouTube and type, "Bad News/Good News" in the search box.

POWER PRAYER: *Dear God, help me to share the good news of the gospel faithfully with my friends so they will make the right choice before they die.*

POWER PASSAGE

"Enter by the narrow gate. For the gate is wide and the way is easy that leads to destruction, and those who enter by it are many. For the gate is narrow and the way is hard that leads to life, and those who find it are few."

Matthew 7:13–14

BEYOND HARPS, CLOUDS, AND GOLD

I grew up in church and became a Christian at an early age, so for many years, I have known I was going to heaven. But honestly, I wasn't that excited about it.

It beats the alternative, but I always thought of heaven as a boring place with a lot of stuffy, religious people. I envisioned it being one long church service with maybe a potluck at the end.

But heaven is so much better than that. Imagine the world's most stunning architecture. Imagine the finest food. Imagine the most beautiful works of art. Imagine a world where everyone gets along, with no war, no disease, no death, and no pain. Imagine a world filled with the greatest scientific advancements. Imagine a world where all of your closest friends can hang out and nobody gets in trouble; nobody has to go home or do work they don't like; and nothing interrupts your joy.

That's heaven. But the coolest part of heaven is the fact that God will be there and we'll get to walk and talk with Him. He'll teach us things we never knew. We'll worship Him in all of His glory.

Here's the thing. Heaven is real. As real as this book and these pages.

Heaven was created for you and for me by a God who loves us without measure. Do me a favor today. Crack your Bible open to Revelation 21 and read about your future home.

Doesn't seem so boring, does it?

Is **heaven** just a **fluffy**, boring place filled with **religious** people?

BOTTOM LINE

Thinking about the home God prepared for us in heaven helps us get through the tough stuff of life (Colossians 3:1–5).

OWN IT

If you're still curious about that place where God has His headquarters, check out *Heaven, Biblical Answers to Common Questions* by Randy Alcorn or search "randy alcorn, heaven" on YouTube.

POWER PRAYER: *Dear God, thank You for preparing heaven for me. Help me to live each day knowing that one day I will live forever with You.*

POWER PASSAGE

He will wipe away every tear from their eyes, and death shall be no more, neither shall there be mourning, nor crying, nor pain anymore, for the former things have passed away.

Revelation 21:4

BEYOND PITCHFORKS, RED SUITS, AND FIRE

G oogle the word *hell* and you'll come up with a few interesting things. Some people think hell is some kind of joke. One late-night comedian said he wants to go to hell because "all his friends are going there." A lot of folks, even some professing Christians, think hell is the creation of angry preachers who just want to scare people into attending church.

But hell is real. It's not a joke. It's not a fun place with friends. It's not a place you'd want your worst enemy to visit.

I know what you're thinking. *If God is loving, how can He send people to hell?* Here's the deal. God didn't actually create hell for people. Hell was created for the devil and his angels (Matthew 25:41). But sin, which began in the Garden of Eden, plunged all of us on a pathway to hell (2 Peter 2:4–9).

God isn't an angry God. In fact, He loved us so much He provided a way out. Jesus Christ is the bridge. He offers not just eternal life in heaven, but an eternal escape from hell.

So how do people end up in hell? They end up there by choice. Instead of embracing God's forgiveness, they choose their own way.

Hell is horrible. The Bible says it is filled with eternal fire (Revelation 21:8). It is lonely. It is dark. It offers no hope. The worst thing about it is that God is not enjoyed there.

I didn't write this today to scare you. I do hope it motivates you to share the good news of the gospel with someone you love (2 Corinthians 5:11).

Why does there have to be a **hell**? **How** could a loving God send people there?

BOTTOM LINE

If hell is real, then we should do all we can to help others escape it.

OWN IT

For more information about that place down below, check out the answer to the question, "Is Hell Real?" by placing that question in the search box at gotquestions.org.

POWER PRAYER: *Dear God, hell sounds like an awful place that we really don't like talking about. But Your Word says that it is real. Thank You for saving me from the horrors of hell. Help me to bring the truth of the gospel to my friends so they can be spared as well.*

POWER PASSAGE

For great is your

steadfast love

toward me;

you have delivered

my soul from

the depths of Sheol.

Psalm 86:13

WATCH OUT FOR THIS GUY

I know what you're thinking. *Great, yesterday he talks about Hell and today he's talking about Satan? That's depressing.*

OK, bear with me. This won't be as bad as you think.

Let's get to the bad news first. An enemy out there wants to see you fail. His name is Satan, and he is real. Here is his story.

Satan was once one of God's top angels. But he got too big for his britches and thought he could do a better job running the universe than God could. So God kicked him out of heaven. Ever since, he's been jealous of God. He takes out his anger by going after God's people. And if you look around the world, you might think that Satan is actually winning.

But here's the rest of the story. Even though Satan is destructive, angry, powerful, and evil, he is no match for God. God has given Satan temporary rule over the world (Ephesians 2:1–2), but God is still in charge (Job 1:6–12). Satan is actually a defeated enemy. Jesus's death on the Cross and His resurrection were the final blow (1 John 3:7–8). One day Satan will be put in eternal fire forever (Revelation 20:10).

In this life, even though Satan will try to tempt you to do evil and accuse you of being worthless to God, the Bible says that we, through the Holy Spirit, have the power to resist him (James 4:1–10). Every time he tempts you to go against God, you can win that battle because God is greater.

See, that wasn't so bad, was it?

An **enemy** out there wants to hurt you. Do you know who he is and how to **defeat** him?

BOTTOM LINE

If you are not aware of the enemy, you won't be aware of his tricks and you'll be a victim of his attacks.

OWN IT

How did Lucifer, God's highest angel, turn into Satan, the arch-enemy of God? Read the sketchy story in Isaiah 14.

POWER PRAYER: *Dear God, help me to resist the charms of the enemy. I realize that I'm powerless against him unless You empower me. I know Satan is strong and cunning and deceitful, but You are stronger. I trust in You.*

POWER PASSAGE

Be sober-minded; be watchful. Your adversary the devil prowls around like a roaring lion, seeking someone to devour.

1 Peter 5:8

DAY 17

THE BIG REMODEL

Jonathan, age 15, recently asked me on Facebook, "If I'm a Christian, why do I still sin? Am I really saved?"

Here's what I told him. There's a big fancy biblical term called *sanctification*. *Sanctification* simply means the process of becoming Christlike or holy. It has three parts.

The first part is *positional sanctification*. That's a mouthful, but what this means is that when you put your faith in Jesus Christ, God doesn't see your sin anymore. He only sees the perfection or righteousness of Jesus Christ (2 Corinthians 5:21). So in the eyes of God, when it comes to your *position* in Christ, you're not a sinner; you're perfect. Pretty cool, eh? But it gets better.

The second part is *progressive sanctification*. God does this work in you while you live this life. It's the process of the Holy Spirit making you more like Jesus Christ (Galatians 4:19). You see, even though God sees us as righteous, we still live in this sinful body. We still sin. But when we choose to follow God, we can become gradually less sinful. We'll never be perfect—until we reach heaven. This leads to the third and coolest part.

The third part is called *permanent sanctification*. Another mouthful. But this is powerful. When we finally go to heaven, God will have completed His work. We'll be perfect and righteous. We won't sin any longer. No more temptation. No more disgusting thoughts. No more disagreements with our loved ones.

That's a really long answer to Jonathan's simple question. Why does he still sin? Why do I still sin? Because we're not yet perfect, but we're in the process of being made perfect.

If I'm a **Christian**, why do I **still sin?**

By the way, Paul, who wrote most of the New Testament, and was one of the greatest missionaries ever, experienced the same struggle with sin (Romans 7:15–20).

BOTTOM LINE

Christians still sin, but they have the Holy Spirit to help them fight temptation.

OWN IT

Check out Paul's honest admission of his own struggle with sin in Romans 7:21–15.

POWER PRAYER: *Dear God, it seems like I mess up every day, maybe every hour. Please forgive my sin and help me to resist temptation. I long for that day when I will be in Heaven with You, made perfect and without sin.*

POWER PASSAGE

And I am sure of this, that he who began a good work in you will bring it to completion at the day of Jesus Christ.

Philippians 1:6

BUT WAIT, THERE'S MORE

I'm back." I'll never forget those words, faxed by Michael Jordan to the news media.

Jordan, our hero in Chicago, was leaving baseball and coming back to play for the Chicago Bulls. When Jordan returned, the Chicago Bulls won three more championships.

Jesus Christ also said, "I'll be back." The first time Jesus came, He came as a Savior. He allowed humans to put Him on the Cross. He paid the penalty for our sin. He was poor. He didn't have a home. Even though He was the Creator, He submitted himself to His creation.

But the next time Jesus comes, it will be different. Jesus will come as the King of the universe. He will take over the world and will rule. All of God's enemies will be defeated.

Christians disagree on the specifics of Jesus's coming. Here is what I believe. Jesus's Second Coming will be in two parts. First, He will take all the Christians out of the world in the Rapture. Then the world will endure seven brutal years of judgment. Then, Jesus will return, and the church will join Him in setting up His kingdom.

Every Christian knows that Jesus Christ is coming again. This is our great hope.

Jesus **promised** that He is **coming again** someday. So **where** is He?

POWER PASSAGE

And if I go

and prepare

a place for you,

I will come again

and will take you

to myself,

that where I am

you may be also.

John 14:3

BOTTOM LINE

Jesus is coming again. What will He find you doing?

OWN IT

If you really want to understand God's plan for the end of time, check out *Are We Living in the End Times?* by Jerry Jenkins and Tim LaHaye.

POWER PRAYER: *Dear Jesus, thank You for coming the first time to save me from my sin. I eagerly wait for Your Second Coming. Help me to live for You until You return.*

DAY 19

TIME FOR THE DUNK TANK

H ere's a question I get a lot. *What is the big deal about baptism? Why does a Christian get up in front of the entire church, in a robe, and get dunked?*

Here's the answer. Before Jesus left the earth, He asked His followers to do two things: be baptized and take communion. Tomorrow we'll talk about communion.

Water baptism is an essential part of following Christ. It symbolizes our identity with Him. We go down into the water (like Jesus going into the grave) and we rise up again (like Jesus rising from the grave).

Some feel that baptism is necessary for salvation, but that's not true. Otherwise, the thief on the cross couldn't have been saved. Jesus told him, *"Today you will be with me in Paradise"* (Luke 23:43). He didn't have time to get down from the cross and get dunked. Baptism is not a part of salvation, but it demonstrates to the rest of the world that you have received salvation. It's a symbol, a sign.

Jesus indicated that it is important for every believer to be baptized. It's a big step of faith. You're telling everyone around you that you identify with Christ and are not ashamed.

Have you been baptized? If not, maybe it's time to talk to your pastor or youth pastor about this important step.

Is **baptism** just an old-fashioned **ritual** or is there something **more** to it?

Go therefore
and make disciples
of all nations,
baptizing them in
the name of the Father
and of the Son
and of the Holy Spirit.

Matthew 28:19

BOTTOM LINE

Being baptized says you're not ashamed to be identified with Christ.

OWN IT

Look up Jesus's command to be baptized in Matthew 28:16–20.

POWER PRAYER: *Dear Jesus, I want to be identified as one of Your followers. Please give me the courage to be baptized and grow in my faith.*

DAY 20

BREAD AND JUICE

Someone once said that a picture is worth a thousand words. I have pictures of my family all over my house. Family pictures decorate my office. They form the wallpaper on my laptop and my iPhone. And my Facebook background has a bunch of them as well.

Think of the people you love the most—your best friend, your parents, your brother or sister. You keep their pictures close because pictures remind you of great times together.

Jesus wanted us to remember Him. So before He left, He gave us a type of picture of Himself. It's a ceremony we call communion. Before He went back to heaven, He told His followers, *"Do this in remembrance of me"* (Luke 22:19).

Each time we break the bread, we remember the broken body of Jesus. It was beaten beyond recognition, His flesh ripped apart. Why? For our sins.

Each time we drink the juice, we remember His blood. The Bible said His blood paid for our sins (Matthew 26:28). Without that blood, we would not have the hope of eternal life.

I've always enjoyed communion. It is a chance to draw closer to God, to confess my sins, and to renew my commitment to Him.

Every church does communion a little differently. Our church celebrates it once a month. I'm not sure how your church does it, but next time you reach for the bread and drink the juice, remember why we do it. It's a picture that's worth well more than a thousand words.

Communion

allows us to travel back to the **Cross** and **remember** Jesus's death.

BOTTOM LINE

Communion service is a special time that brings us back mentally to the Cross where our sins were forgiven.

OWN IT

Next time your church shares communion, take time to reflect on the death of Jesus Christ. Look up these important passages in the Bible: Matthew 26:26–29; 1 Corinthians 11:17–34.

POWER PRAYER: *Dear Jesus, thank You for willingly going to the Cross to suffer my punishment. Your love purchased my freedom. Your blood covered my sin. Your sacrifice gave me new life.*

POWER PASSAGE

For as often as you eat this bread and drink the cup, you proclaim the Lord's death until he comes.

1 Corinthians 11:26

DOCTRINE—
Knowing What You Believe and Why

Talk About It
(with your friends, your parents, or your pastor)

> *How do our beliefs affect the way we live?*

> *How are your beliefs being challenged every day in the culture (popular teachings at school, movies, music, books, online)?*

> *Did you have any questions about any essential beliefs?*

Go Deeper
Here are a few resources to help you investigate the ideas we talked about for the last 20 days.

Web sites:

gotquestions.org

seanmcdowell.org

Books:

Moody Handbook of Theology

The Five Minute Theologian
　　—Rick Cornish

The Case for Christ—Student Edition
　　—Lee Strobel

Jesus, Dead or Live?
　　Evidence for the Resurrection—Teen Edition
　　—Sean McDowell

SECTION TWO

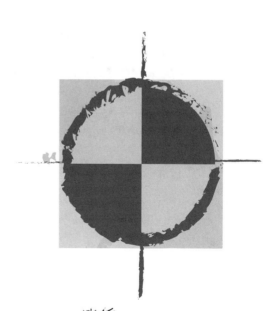

DECISIONS—
HOW TO MAKE GOOD CHOICES

THE BIG QUESTION

Emma came home early from school. Her mom was on the phone with a friend.

"Yeah, I don't know about Emma. She just doesn't seem to have any direction or drive. I don't know what kind of career she's going to have."

Emma wasn't supposed to hear those words. But she did and each one was a dagger to her heart. Tears streaked down her face. *Mom really feels that way? Why doesn't she believe in me?*

Do you ever feel like Emma? Like nobody believes in you? Sometimes those closest to us can't see past our mistakes. They only seem to catch us when we mess up.

I've got good news for you. Someone believes in you. God does. Just when your family, your friends, your teachers have written you off, God says, "I love you and I believe in you." What's more, He has a great plan for your life.

Not a plan to see how spectacularly you can fail. Not a plan that has you living an uninteresting life. Not the plan that everyone *seems* to have in mind for you. No, the Bible says God's plan is brimming with adventure and hope.

Do you want that? I do. So, chin up. God's opinion of you matters most.

When
others doubt
you, hang on
to **God's promise**
to give you a future
and a **hope**.

BOTTOM LINE

Even when nobody believes in you, God believes in you and has a plan for your life.

OWN IT

Write Jeremiah 29:11 on a sticky note and post it in a prominent place, like your locker or your mirror or the dashboard of your car.

POWER PRAYER: *Dear God, thank You for loving me without reservation. I don't totally know the plan You have for my life, but I am grateful that You believe in my future, even when others don't.*

POWER PASSAGE

For I know the plans I have for you, declares the LORD, plans for welfare and not for evil, to give you a future and a hope.

Jeremiah 29:11

DAY 22

HE KNOWS WHO YOU ARE

W hen somebody broke into her locker, stole her diary, and passed it around school, Crystal felt violated. Her personal thoughts, her secret longings, her hidden fears were now broadcast for public consumption. Could she ever face her friends again? Would they still like her?

Like Crystal, we all have secrets that we hope nobody discovers. That's why we try so hard to keep them locked in a safe place in our hearts or with friends who we know we can trust. But Someone sees what no one else sees.

Psalm 139 says God knows everything about us. Our thoughts, our intentions, our habits and quirks, and our words.

This might scare you or it might comfort you. It could be scary, because we know what happens when someone gets a hold of our secrets. They might see us in a different light. They might stop loving us. They might even try to use this information against us.

But God doesn't do that. He's not like humans. He knows everything about us and yet He still loves us. Isn't that incredible?

God understands you in a way nobody else can. He is intimately aware of every detail of your life. God knows who you are. God knows what makes you tick. God understands your needs, your desires, your dreams.

That's why God is your very best friend. You can trust Him with your life.

A God who **knows everything** about you is a God who **knows what is best** for you.

BOTTOM LINE

A God who knows everything about you knows what's best for you.

OWN IT

Reread Psalm 139. Personalize it by putting your name in each place where the psalmist says "me" or "mine."

POWER PRAYER: *God, I know You know the end from the beginning, I know You know everything about me. Thank You for loving me in spite of me.*

POWER PASSAGE

O Lord, you have searched me and known me! You know when I sit down and when I rise up; you discern my thoughts from afar. You search out my path and my lying down and are acquainted with all my ways. Even before a word is on my tongue, behold, O Lord, you know it altogether.

Psalm 139:1–4

DAY 23

HE WANTS TO LEAD YOU

When I was a kid, the grocery store seemed like the largest place on the planet. So losing my mom was a frightening experience. I'd be gazing at the Cap'n Crunch cereal boxes when all of a sudden, Mom was gone. I'd scream at the top of my lungs. Then I'd hear her say, "Daniel, I'm over here." One aisle over. My fears were relieved.

David didn't like being alone either. He spent many hours on the hillsides, just him and the sheep. But he knew he wasn't alone. God was there with him.

David said there was nowhere he could go to escape God's presence (Psalm 139:7). He could travel to the ends of the universe. He could fly into the heavens. He could swim to the deepest parts of the ocean. He could endure the darkest night. Still God was always there.

Some find that frightening. David found it comforting. I find it comforting. Because wherever we go, whatever life brings us, God is always there and He wants to take our hand and lead us.

Sometimes, like a fidgety little child, we're tempted to squeeze our hands away from God's grip. But being alone in this world is frightening. It's better to know He's guiding you.

There is **nowhere** you can go to escape **God's presence**.

POWER PASSAGE

Even there

your hand

shall lead me,

and your right hand

shall hold me.

Psalm 139:10

BOTTOM LINE

If you know God, then you're never alone. You have Him to guide you through the darkest times of your life.

OWN IT

Read Jacob's story of loneliness on page 58 of *Teen People of the Bible.*

POWER PRAYER: *Dear God, sometimes I feel very alone. I feel as if nobody cares and nobody knows the struggles I'm facing. Thank You for being my friend. Hold my hand and guide me.*

DAY 24

HE KNOWS WHAT YOU ARE

There is nothing as hurtful as the sting of rejection. Parents who whisper cruel and painful words. A boyfriend or a girlfriend who leaves you for somebody he or she thinks is better looking or more gifted. The pain runs deep and hard.

Centuries ago, another unwanted teenager experienced the pain of rejection. While his brothers were praised for their height, their good looks, and their accomplishments on the battlefield, David was tossed aside. His own father was embarrassed by him. But David discovered something powerful. He discovered that what God thought about him was more important than any human opinion. What did God think about him? The same thing He thinks about you. You're a unique and precious creation.

Maybe you feel as if life is worthless and hopeless. I want you to know that you have a Creator who designed you with a purpose. Before you were born, God wanted you and loved you. You were *"fearfully and wonderfully made."* The Creator formed your body, your personality, your character with painstaking precision. Nothing about you is accidental.

Ignore those cruel words of rejection. Anyone who tells you that you are insignificant, unworthy, and unloved is a liar and out of step with God's will.

The only opinion that matters is the opinion of the One who created you. He loves you just the way you are.

What does
God think
about **my life**?

BOTTOM LINE

God's opinion of you is the only opinion that matters.

OWN IT

Read David's story in 1 Samuel 16.

POWER PRAYER: *Dear God, I want to thank You for creating me in a special unique way. Help me to filter out the negative messages that keep me from embracing Your unique call upon my life.*

POWER PASSAGE

I praise you,

for I am fearfully and

wonderfully made.

Wonderful

are your works;

my soul knows it

very well.

Psalm 139:14

DAY 25

BETTER THAN GYM CLASS

I was quite possibly the least athletic guy in high school, so when it came time to pick teams in gym class or pickup basketball games, I was the nerdy kid with big, bad, plastic glasses who got picked last.

But something happened before my junior year. I grew three inches and lost 30 pounds. Suddenly, I wasn't the last person picked. I was one of the first.

To be chosen is a special feeling. Whether it's gym class or debate team or the cheerleading squad. You feel like you're on top of the world.

If you are a Christian, the Bible says that you are chosen. Chosen by the God of the Universe. We read in Ephesians 1:3–4 that people who believe in Jesus Christ don't just wander into God's family randomly. No, God had a plan that included you, even before He laid the foundation of the world. He wanted you to be a part of His grand family.

God chose you for a unique purpose. That purpose is to make a difference in this world by being different. By being holy and blameless and to show God's glory to the world through your life.

That honor is way better than being chosen first in gym class.

You are
not random,
   you are chosen.
Chosen
by Almighty God.

Blessed be the God

and Father of

our Lord Jesus Christ,

who has blessed us

in Christ with every

spiritual blessing in the

heavenly places,

even as he chose us

in him before the

foundation of the world,

that we should be

holy and blameless

before him.

Ephesians 1:3–4

BOTTOM LINE

You are not in God's family by accident. You were chosen by God before the world began.

OWN IT

Read Ephesians 1:3; 2 Peter 2:9; Genesis 1:26; Psalm 139. Make a list of all the characteristics God has for His people.

POWER PRAYER: *Dear God, Sometimes I feel left out or unwanted by certain groups of people. Thank You for choosing me to be a part of Your family.*

DAY 26

MOVIN' ON UP

In the movie, *The Ultimate Gift*, Jason Stevens is a young man who can't wait to get his hands on a large fortune from his rich grandfather who just died. But before Jason saw a single dollar, he had to finish 12 tasks designed to teach him a little bit about life.

I think most of us would do 12 tasks if it meant we'd get a ton of money. We'd probably do 100 tasks. I'm guessing that isn't happening anytime soon, though.

What if I told you that you have an inheritance waiting for you? Not a fancy car or a million-dollar check but something much greater. It's an unlimited treasure given to us when we join God's family.

The Bible says we've been adopted into God's family, which means we are treated like an honored son or daughter, a prince or princess. God is ready to unlock the vault and shower His children with everything good.

What exactly does this mean? It means you're not alone in this world. You have the God of the Universe holding nothing back from your life. He's on your side.

How do God's gifts help us every day? Well, He gives us grace when we mess up. He gives us peace in the midst of our storms, or life challenges. He gives us strength to live out our faith. He gives us love for those who are unlovable. He gives us joy when we're not feeling very joyful. He offers wisdom for making tough choices.

Because you are His child, God gives these gifts in unlimited supply. That sounds a lot better than a million dollars or a new car, doesn't it?

What does it mean to be a **member** of **God's family**?

BOTTOM LINE

When you come to Christ, God gives you an unlimited treasure.

OWN IT

Check out the movie, *The Ultimate Gift*.

POWER PRAYER: *Dear God, thank You for gifts You give every single day—riches like wisdom and grace, peace and joy, love and forgiveness.*

POWER PASSAGE

He predestined us for adoption as sons through Jesus Christ, according to the purpose of his will.

Ephesians 1:5

DAY 27

YOU'RE ACCEPTED

"You're accepted." Those two words may be the most important words you ever hear. Sometimes they are printed on a letter from a university or an employer. Other times those words are implied by a group of friends who allow you into their circle.

Quite often, though, we hear the opposite words. Nobody ever says, "You're not accepted," but a person's actions imply it. A shrug of the shoulder. A rolling of the eyes. An unanswered phone call or email.

There are all kinds of reasons for being rejected. Your weight. Your culture. Your family background. Your past. Your lack of talent. The way you dress.

We work so hard to get accepted. We change our clothing. We change our habits. We change our music. And yet, sometimes it's just not good enough.

If today you're feeling like nobody wants you, know this: you don't have to try hard to gain God's acceptance. He's already accepted you for who you are.

Jesus's sacrifice on the Cross paved the way for God to accept you. He doesn't see your sin; He only sees the perfection of Jesus Christ. You're accepted by the Creator, the one who knows the beginning and the end.

Take a moment and let that huge truth sink in. The One who made everything—designed the entire universe—accepts and loves you.

God has **not rejected** you. He's
accepted
you forever.

BOTTOM LINE

You are accepted and loved by the Creator of the Universe.

OWN IT

To really discover how much God loves you, check out *Cherished* by Chandra Peele.

POWER PRAYER: *Dear Jesus, thank You for dying on the Cross and paying the way for my acceptance by God as one of His children. I want to grow closer to You and know You like You want to be known.*

POWER PASSAGE

To the praise of his glorious grace, with which he has blessed us in the Beloved. In him we have redemption through his blood, the forgiveness of our trespasses, according to the riches of his grace.

Ephesians 1:6–7

SOMETHING WORTH DYING FOR

R oss McGinnis was a 19–year-old army private from Knox, Pennsylvania. He had his entire life ahead of him, a bright future once he returned to the United States after a tour of duty in Iraq.

But Ross never returned. That's because he made a split-second decision, an act of courage that saved the lives of his four buddies. Perched in the gunner's hatch of a Humvee, he saw a grenade fly past him into the truck where his friends sat. Ross quickly shouted a warning, but instead of jumping out to his own safety, he jumped into the truck and onto the grenade.

Ross lost his life that day, but he saved the lives of his friends. He was later awarded the Medal of Honor by President George W. Bush at an emotional ceremony at the White House.

Jesus said this is the highest form of love—to lay your life down for your friends. Jesus would know, because later He would lay His life down for you and for me. We are His friends. And He calls us to do the same.

Most of us won't ever face the decision Ross McGinnis faced. We'll never have the opportunity to sacrifice our own lives for the lives of those we love.

But God calls us to do something even greater. That is to live our faith. By living each day for Him, we are sacrificing ourselves—our selfish needs and wants—for the good of others. This is the call of every Christian. And it is the call of God upon your life.

There is **no greater call** than to lay your life down for a cause you **believe** in.

POWER PASSAGE

Greater love

has no one than this,

that someone

lay down his life

for his friends.

John 15:13

BOTTOM LINE

Giving your life for a greater cause is the call of every young person.

OWN IT

Ask yourself today, in what ways, large and small, is God calling me to give my life for the good of others? What needy people in my life can I serve today?

POWER PRAYER: *Dear God, help me to answer the call of the crucified life. Give me strength to serve others, to lay my life down for the lives of others. Thank You for Your example in willingly surrendering Your life for my freedom.*

DAY 29

YOU MIGHT BE THE CHANGE

I'm too young.

I just want to have fun.

There's not much I can do anyway.

These are the excuses I hear all the time from teens who don't think they can make a difference in the world.

Thousands of years ago, there was a young man with the same set of lame excuses. His name was Jeremiah. He loved God. He grew up in a God-respecting home. He was comfortable just blending in. But God had something different for Jeremiah.

God told this young person that he would be a prophet—a teller of truth—to a generation of people who didn't want to follow God. His words would not be taken kindly. He would be persecuted for his faith. He was called to be different, to be a light in the darkness.

Is God calling you to be a truth-teller in your generation? Our world needs young men and young women willing to stand up for the truth. Young people are increasingly rejecting the truth of God's Word. They are being seduced by the lies of the world and the enemy. This generation needs truth-tellers, Jeremiahs willing to stand for the truth.

Before He was born, God had laid out the plans for Jeremiah's life. He created him and equipped him to be a difference-maker. So it is with you. Everything God has given you, your unique talents and abilities and gifts, were given for one purpose—to glorify God in your generation.

Jeremiah answered the call. Will you?

Is God raising **you**
up to be a
difference-maker
in your generation?

POWER PASSAGE

"Before I formed you

in the womb

I knew you, and

before you were born

I consecrated you;

I appointed you

a prophet

to the nations."

Jeremiah 1:5

BOTTOM LINE

God is calling you to be a Jeremiah in your generation.

OWN IT

If you want to read about a modern-day Jeremiah, reach the story of Zach Hunter, a teen who has fought the human slave trade. His story is told in his book, *Be the Change.*

POWER PRAYER: *Dear God, help me to be a Jeremiah in my generation. Help me to stand up and be a truth-teller, to make a difference for You.*

DARE TO BE DIFFERENT

C hase doesn't go to parties where there are no adults around. Jenny doesn't allow herself to be alone in a car with a guy. Josh always tries to show up to football practice on time, even if everyone else is late.

Why are they making these choices? Everyone is going to the party. All the girls go out alone with guys in cars. Everyone is ragging on Coach. But as my mom used to say, "Dan, you're not everybody."

A follower of Christ is not everybody. He tries to *be* different so he can *make* a difference. The world offers conformity—sameness. Be like us, do like us, hang with us. They want you to give up your individuality. Without realizing it, you slowly become a slave to the world's way of doing things.

Jesus offers something completely different. Jesus offers transformation. He desires to radically change us, from the inside out. That transformation frees us up to be true to the person God uniquely intended each of us to be. That's the beauty of the church. It's not a group of Christian clones, but a diverse family, filled with people of all shapes and sizes and preferences and colors and races and gifts.

Have you looked at the world lately? Everyone's the same. They read the same books, watch the same TV shows, and eat the same food . I don't want that. You don't want that.

God has something better. You're not everybody. You're somebody unique in Christ.

You make a
difference
in the world—
by being different
from the world.

POWER PASSAGE

I appeal to you

therefore, brothers,

by the mercies of God,

to present your bodies

as a living sacrifice,

holy and acceptable

to God, which is your

spiritual worship.

Romans 12:1

BOTTOM LINE

The world offers sameness, but Jesus offers radical change.

OWN IT

Brett and Alex Harris are two teens determined to make a difference. They challenge other teens in their book, *Do Hard Things* and on their Web site, therebelution.com.

POWER PRAYER: *Dear God, help me to make a difference in this world, by being different and preaching the truth of the gospel to my generation. I know I can only do this in Your power.*

CAN YOU HEAR ME NOW?

C handra flipped through the brochure for the missions trip to Ecuador. Her heart ached at the stories of children who roamed the streets in search of food. Then she read the statistics, showing how many people in that country had not heard the gospel message.

What can I do? I'm only one person, she thought. Then she read the words of Isaiah, who had answered God's call. Five simple words, *"Here am I. Send me."* Chandra bowed her head. With tears, she prayed, *Dear God. I'm only one person. I have limited talents and abilities. But I want to be a part of that difference. Send me.*

Robert Moffat, Scottish missionary to Africa, said, "I have seen, at different times, the smoke of a thousand villages—villages whose people are without Christ, without God, and without hope in the world."

Will you be the answer to that need? Is your heart burdened to share God's love with those who have never heard? Are you willing to say, "Here am I. Send me"?

God may call you to the Africa, or he may call you to America. He may call you to be a missionary, a pastor, a youth pastor, or He may call you to be a police officer, a doctor, a grocery sacker, or custodian.

Wherever you go, whatever you end up doing, your mission for God is full-time. You're to be a light in a dark world. An agent of change in a world gone wrong.

The **voice of God** is calling.
Are you **listening**?

POWER PASSAGE

And I heard the
voice of the Lord saying,
"Whom shall I send,
and who will go for us?"
Then I said,
"Here am I! Send me."

Isaiah 6:8

BOTTOM LINE

God is calling. Are you listening?

OWN IT

Check out the movie, *The End of the Spear*, which features the story of Nate Saint, one of five missionaries who gave their lives to share Christ in Ecuador.

POWER PRAYER: *Dear God, open my heart to be sensitive to Your call. I want to serve You wherever You call. I want my life to be a witness to a lost world.*

DAY 32

THE BIG FAT MYSTERY

OK, so you really know what you believe, and you want to follow God, but how in the world do you know what He wants you to do?

A lot of folks think God's will is a big, vague mystery, buried in a secret lockbox. They float through life in a haze of confusion, waiting for this grand mystery to be revealed. They're afraid to try or do anything that might *not* be God's will.

It doesn't have to be that hard. So how do we figure out what God wants us to do? We begin with God Himself. Today's power passage from Psalm 37:4–5 gives us two instructions. Delight. Commit.

First, you fall in love with God and build that relationship with Him; you come to know Him so well that His desires become your desires. He plants His will in the deepest part of your soul, so that you won't have to guess where to go and what to do. You'll just do the sort of things God wants.

Then, you commit yourself to your God-given passions. You trust that God knows what He is doing. You work hard and pursue every opportunity to grow. And if you do this, the psalmist says that God *"will act."*

See, it's really not such a big fat mystery after all.

Is the **Bible** just **another book** or is there **something more** to it?

POWER PASSAGE

Delight yourself in the LORD, and he will give you the desires of your heart. Commit your way to the LORD; trust in him, and he will act.

Psalm 37:4–5

BOTTOM LINE

Fall in love with God and He'll show you His will.

OWN IT

Reread Psalm 37. Spend some time reflecting on God's truth. Ask yourself these questions: *Am I delighting in God? Am I seeking Him and Him alone? What obstacles keep me from Him?*

POWER PRAYER: *Dear God, I want to delight in You. I want to know You. I want to walk with You. Please remove any obstacles to my delighting in You. Implant Your purpose in the deepest part of my heart.*

DAY 33

THE 90/10 RULE

People say, "If God would just write down what He wants me to do, I'd do it." Guess what? He has. Everything necessary that God wanted you to know, He put in His Word. He didn't hold anything back. It's the Creator's instruction manual. It's a conversation between you and God who loves you.

I have a 90/10 rule. Answers for 90 percent of the questions we have about our future and about our life are written in the pages of Scripture. They are easy questions we like to make difficult. As for the other 10 percent—those specific questions about what college to attend, whom to date, what car to buy, etc.—the Bible allows us freedom of choice. Instead of laying out the details, it tells us how to be the kind of believers we ought to be so as to know how to make the best choices.

Today let's focus on the 90 percent. Here are a few basic instructions God gives:

1. Attend church regularly. (Hebrews 10:25)

2. Live a life of prayer. (1 Thessalonians 5:17)

3. Regularly meditate on the Word. (Psalm 119:11)

4. Share your faith. (Colossians 4:4–6)

5. Serve others. (Romans 15:2)

6. Save sex for marriage. (Hebrews 13:4)

7. Forgive. (Matthew 18:21–22)

8. Marry someone who is a believer. (2 Corinthians 6:14)

9. Watch who influences you. (1 Corinthians 15:33)

If the Bible is really **God's Word,** maybe it says something about **how to live** my life.

And that's just a smidgen. So start with what you know and let God fill in the details. Because if you can't handle the 90 percent, you'll never figure out the 10 percent.

BOTTOM LINE

Knowing God's will isn't as hard as we make it.

OWN IT

Check out my article on crosswalk .com, entitled, "Stop Wrestling, Start Serving: The Non-Mystery of God's Will."

POWER PRAYER: *Dear God, help me to do what I know is Your will. Help me to live the Word of God, applying its wisdom and truths to my daily life.*

POWER PASSAGE

And how from childhood you have been acquainted with the sacred writings, which are able to make you wise for salvation through faith in Christ Jesus. All Scripture is breathed out by God and profitable for teaching, for reproof, for correction, and for training in righteousness, that the man of God may be competent, equipped for every good work.

2 Timothy 3:15–17

PASSIONS AND PURPOSE

OK, so, you're following Christ. You're reading the Word, but you still have a few questions. You've searched from Genesis to Revelation and you're not seeing any information about what college to attend, which job to take, what girl to ask out. Now you're thinking, *OK, is there a secret book of the Bible somebody hid from me?*

No secret book. But that doesn't mean you're on your own with those difficult decisions.

So how do we find answers? Well, today's passage gives us some guidance. If you're walking with the Lord and your heart is closely aligned with His, then His desires will be your desires.

Start by asking yourself a few questions. What do you enjoy doing? What would you like to do with your life? What gifts and talents do you see in yourself? What gifts and talents do others see in you?

Maybe you enjoy writing or speaking. Maybe you are an artist or a musician. Maybe you are skilled with your hands or enjoy working with children.

The unique package that is you—your gifts, your personality, your passions—wasn't put there by accident. God purposely made you who you are. So use your gifts, your personality, your talents for His glory.

Then watch God direct your steps.

If your heart is close to **God's heart**, then He will implant in your heart **His desires**.

BOTTOM LINE

Your passions, your gifts, your talents were uniquely given by God to fulfill His will in your life.

OWN IT

Take a sheet of paper and divide it into three columns titled: My Talents, My Passions, My Gifts. Write down your answers in each area. Show your list to someone you trust, like your teachers or your parents or your friends, and get their opinion.

POWER PRAYER: *Dear God, thank You for giving me the unique package of gifts and talents and passions that make me who I am. Help me to follow the desires You have put in my heart so my life glorifies You.*

POWER PASSAGE

Delight yourself in the LORD, and he will give you the desires of your heart. Commit your way to the LORD; trust in him, and he will act.

Psalm 37:4–5

OPPORTUNITY IS KNOCKING

Archery was always a big part of summer camp. I remember how hard it was to keep the bow steady, thread the arrow through the string, sight the target, and then let go. It was hard to get all that right and hit the bull's eye.

Many people think God's will is like a bull's eye. Either you hit it straight on or you miss it. That sounds really spiritual, but what happens if you miss your one chance? What happens if that one person you were supposed to marry marries someone else? Are you stuck with plan B?

I don't think God works that way. If he does, then we're all on plan B. Or maybe plan C, D, and F.

We talked yesterday about pursuing your God-given passions and gifts. Once you do that, God will open up doors and opportunities. It may be an internship in a business or ministry. It may be a special class at school. It might be a missions trip or a service opportunity.

You may not always be 100 percent sure what to do, but don't let that paralyze you into doing nothing. Investigate opportunities in your areas of interest. Pray over them. Then pursue opportunities as they are presented.

Above all, soak your dreams and decisions with prayer. Ask God to help you pursue open doors.

If God is the Creator and He has given you **special passions** and **gifts** and **talents**, then wouldn't He have a plan to use those for **His purpose**?

BOTTOM LINE

God works through open doors and opportunities.

OWN IT

Revisit the list you created yesterday (Day 34) and add another column titled: My Opportunities. Now think of opportunities you can pursue in areas where you are both passionate and talented.

POWER PRAYER: *Dear God, I don't know exactly what Your will is. Help me to see every opportunity as an open door. Give me the courage to walk through those doors. Help my life to glorify You.*

POWER PASSAGE

For a wide door

for effective work

has opened to me,

and there are

many adversaries.

1 Corinthians 16:9

WISE GUYS

Mrs. Birginal was one of those teachers who always knew what to say. One day after reading an essay I wrote for English Lit, she pulled me aside. "Dan, I really think you've got some talent here. You should write more."

Those words may not have seemed like much to Mrs. Birginal, but they were gold to me. At the time, I didn't really know what I was good at and where my life was headed.

Mrs. Birginal gave me direction, and I'll never forget her kindness. Others came along and confirmed what Mrs. Birginal said. I'm so glad I listened, because God seemed to bring those people along at just the right time.

I hope you have people like this in your life. A teacher, a coach, a youth pastor, a neighbor. Someone a little older, a little wiser, who has walked this road before.

If you don't, find someone. It should be a person who walks with God and lives their life to serve others. Ask to sit down and talk with them for a while. Maybe even offer to buy them coffee or do a special favor for them, like cleaning their house or mowing their lawn.

It may not be the coolest thing for a teenager to talk to an older person, but you'd be surprised at how many things you have in common. Plus, the Bible says that there is wisdom in seeking the input of "many advisors." And wisdom is the fuel you need for a life of impact.

Listening to older people might be a **good idea,** especially if they can help you **avoid** a lifetime of **problems**.

BOTTOM LINE

The wisdom of others may help us discover our gifts and talents.

OWN IT

Ask yourself: *Is there a teacher, a coach, a youth pastor who can help me figure out God's will for my life? How can I glean wisdom from their life?*

POWER PRAYER: *Dear God, thank You for the people you have placed in my life who can give me direction and wisdom about my future. Help me to heed their wisdom so I can live a life of impact.*

POWER PASSAGE

Without counsel

plans fail,

but with many advisors

they succeed.

Proverbs 15:22

DAY 37

HAVE YOU UNWRAPPED YOUR GIFT?

W e often use the phrase, "So and so is really gifted." What does that mean? Does that mean some have gifts and others don't?

Did you know every single child of God has been given at least one spiritual gift? The Bible calls them "grace gifts." They are different from talents. They are special abilities, given by the Holy Spirit, that allow you to serve others and serve God.

God graces some with the ability to preach and teach and lead others. He graces some with the ability to work with their hands. He gives some a special knack for giving, either financially or with their time.

What is the difference between a spiritual gift and a natural talent? Everyone has some talent, but only believers have spiritual gifts. And while talents can be used to glorify God or to glorify ourselves, spiritual gifts are specifically used to build up the faith of others in the church (Romans 12; Ephesians 4; 1 Corinthians 12).

How do you find your spiritual gift? It's simple. Start serving others in the church. See where you naturally fit in. Discover where God uses you the most. Other believers will notice your gift as they see God unfold His purposes through your life.

God has given you
a special **gift** that
enables you to
serve others
in His church.

> Now there are
> varieties of gifts,
> but the same Spirit;
> and there are
> varieties of service,
> but the same Lord;
> and there are
> varieties of activities,
> but it is the same God
> who empowers them
> all in everyone.
>
> **1 Corinthians 12:4–6**

BOTTOM LINE

Spiritual gifts are gifts given from God for the purpose of helping other believers.

OWN IT

Read Romans 12:3–8; 1 Corinthians 12:4–11; Ephesians 4:11–13. These passages list the various spiritual gifts of believers.

POWER PRAYER: *Dear God, please reveal to me my spiritual gifts. Help me to apply them, with Your power, to help serve others in Your church.*

SAMSON, SURRENDER, AND SECOND CHANCES

There he stood, shamed and broken. He'd lived a life of regret. Samson was so thoroughly gifted and yet so easily tempted. There are a lot of hard lessons to learn from his life, lessons every young person should heed. But perhaps the best lesson from Samson's life is that God never gives up on anyone. He is a God of second chances.

Maybe the last few days have overwhelmed you. We've talked about direction and surrender and gifts and talents and choosing the right path. You might be thinking to yourself, *Yeah, that's great, but what if I screw up?*

Know this: You will make mistakes. You will fail God. You will make wrong choices. You will do this because you're a sinner. And the enemy wants the shame and guilt of bad choices to paralyze your future.

Samson's life tells us that it's never too late to be used by God. God used this broken man, at the end of his life, to win a great victory for Israel.

Have you messed up? Admit it. Today is the day to surrender to God and start walking that straight path again.

Is anyone **beyond** the **grace** of a loving **God**?

POWER PASSAGE

And Samson said, "Let me die with the Philistines." Then he bowed with all his strength, and the house fell upon the lords and upon all the people who were in it. So the dead whom he killed at his death were more than those whom he had killed during his life. Then his brothers and all his family came down and took him and brought him up and buried him between Zorah and Eshtaol in the tomb of Manoah his father. He had judged Israel twenty years.

Judges 16:30–31

BOTTOM LINE

God is the God of second, third, fourth, and a zillion chances.

OWN IT

Read Samson's story on pages 34–39 of *Teen People of the Bible*.

POWER PRAYER: *Dear God, I know I am unworthy of Your grace. But I realize that You have forgiven my sins, You've buried my past, and You can give me strength to live for You each day of my life.*

DAY 39

LIVING A LEGACY

On January 8, 1956, Jim Elliot, Ed McCully, Roger Youderian, Pete Fleming, and Nate Saint were murdered in the jungles of Ecuador. They had left the comforts of their American life to bring the light of the gospel to one of the most violent and backward tribes in the world, the *Huaorani* Indian tribe known as the Aucas.

Jim Elliot was 35 years old and recently married. His death seemed like one more senseless tragedy. But was it? A note in his journal reveals the purpose of Jim's life. "He is no fool who gives what he cannot keep to gain what he cannot lose."

Jim and his four buddies left a lasting imprint on their generation and generations to come. Thousands of missionaries were inspired by their story and went to the missions field. And today, many of those very same Aucas have believed I and passed down the gospel to the next generations. It completely changed the tribe from being one of the most brutally violent to one of the most peaceful tribes on the planet. The effect of these young men's lives was profound.

What about you? What will your legacy be? You might say, *I'm young. I've got my whole life ahead of me.* But life moves fast. Nobody knows when it is his or her time. And so old or young, we must ask ourselves, What are we leaving behind? What will we be known for?

God has **blessed** you with a unique package of **talents, gifts, and circumstances.** What are you **doing** with it?

BOTTOM LINE

It's not the length of your life that matters, but its impact.

OWN IT

Read the classic book by Elisabeth Elliot, *Through Gates of Splendor.*

POWER PRAYER: *Dear God, I surrender my life to You. As long as I live, I want to be devoted to You, so that those who don't know You will hear of Your saving grace.*

POWER PASSAGE

Everyone to whom much was given, of him much will be required, and from him to whom they entrusted much, they will demand the more.

Luke 12:48

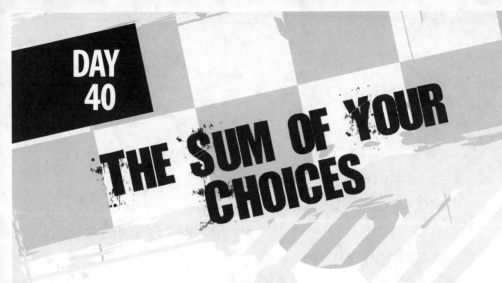

DAY 40

THE SUM OF YOUR CHOICES

The message penetrated my heart. The music reached deep into my soul. Tears flowed down my face.

It was the last night of camp and the speaker had powerfully moved me to action. I couldn't sit in my seat any longer. I walked forward, committing my life to the service of the Lord. It was a big commitment, but one I intended to keep.

I thought this was the hard part. But it was the easy part. The hard part was living every day. I discovered that by Monday, I was tempted to do the same old things, to live the same old way I had lived before that last night at camp.

The lesson I learned is that while life is full of big commitments, those commitments are fulfilled by a daily surrender. Every day we have to "walk the aisle" and lay down our lives at the altar of His will.

The big choices in life are backed up by millions of little choices, made day after day, in the grind of daily life. In other words, the decision to follow Christ begins today, right now where you are and continues throughout every day of your life.

Your life
is the sum of a million little **choices**.

BOTTOM LINE

Your life is the sum of thousands of little daily choices.

OWN IT

Ask yourself these questions this week: *What good choices am I making every day? What poor choices am I making? What different choices can I start making?*

POWER PRAYER: *Dear God, I surrender my choices to You every day. Help me to walk closely with You, help my attitudes and decisions to glorify You today.*

POWER PASSAGE

For it is

precept upon precept,

precept upon precept,

line upon line,

line upon line,

here a little,

there a little.

Isaiah 28:10

DECISIONS—
How to Make Good Choices

Talk About It
(with your friends, your parents, or your pastor)

Who does God say I am?

How do I know I can trust God and His plans for my life?

How do I discover God's plan for my life?

What is the highest form of love?

Go Deeper
Here are a few resources to help you investigate the ideas we talked about for the last 20 days.

Web sites:
therebelution.com

girltalkhome.com

realteenfaith.com

tddm.org

devozine.com

Books:
Teen People of the Bible—Daniel Darling

Do Hard Things—Alex and Brett Harris

A Young Woman After God's Own Heart
—Elizabeth George

A Young Man After God's Own Heart
—Jim George

Great Love (for Guys)—Chandra Peele

Great Love (for Girls)—Chandra Peele

SECTION THREE

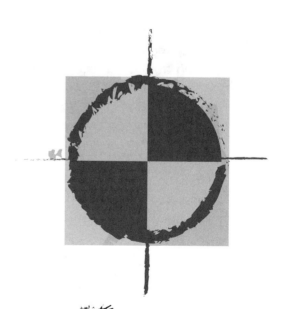

DIRECTION —
WHAT SHOULD I DO WITH MY LIFE?

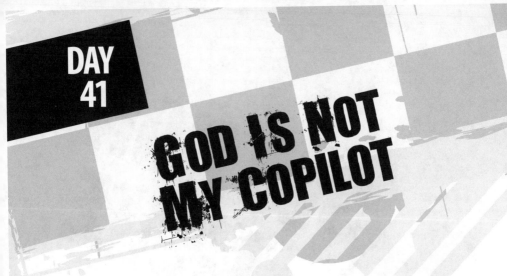

DAY 41

GOD IS NOT MY COPILOT

I don't put them on my car, but I enjoy reading bumper stickers. My new neighbor has one that reads—in big, bold print—"God Loves You," but in tiny print reads, "everyone else thinks you're a jerk!" I'm still laughing at that one.

One I see a lot has me puzzled. It reads, "God is my copilot." Sounds good, but is that a good way to live? I'm not sure God is interested in being the copilot of your life. He'd rather be your pilot.

In fact, when we take our hands off the steering wheel and slide out of the driver's seat, we give God the freedom to steer us in the way that He knows is best for us.

Today, the words of Solomon, the wisest young man who ever lived, ring true, *"In all your ways acknowledge God, and he will make straight your paths."*

What does it mean to acknowledge God? It's making a vow that you will consider God in every single choice you make. *What does God think about my boyfriend or girlfriend? What does God think about the college I'm considering? What does God think about this new job?*

I must admit, this is an easy thing to write, but a hard thing to do. Opening up your life to the lordship of Christ swims against the tide. It might not make you popular.

But you'll go through life with wisdom others don't have, and you'll avoid the pitfalls of a life without God's guidance.

Maybe we should put that on a bumper sticker.

Where is God
in the **choices**
you make?

POWER PASSAGE

In all your ways
acknowledge him,
and he will make
straight your paths.

Proverbs 3:6

BOTTOM LINE

God wants to be involved in every choice you make.

OWN IT

Take a sheet of paper and write down some of your most important choices. Each day this week, pray over one particular choice, asking God to reveal His will in that area.

POWER PRAYER: *Dear God, I'm often tempted to do things my way, but I know Your way is best. I surrender my choices to You. Please show me Your will in the choices I make.*

DAY 42

HELP IS ON THE WAY

Imagine if God came to you one day and said, "You have one wish. You can have anything you want." What would you ask for?

Money? Good looks? A stable family? Athletic ability?

There was a young man who once had this opportunity. His name was Solomon. He literally had the world at his fingertips, and God asked him this very question. But you'd be surprised at Solomon's request.

He asked for . . . wisdom. Why wisdom? Doesn't that sound kind of boring?

Actually, Solomon was on to something. The Bible says wisdom is the most important thing in life. Wisdom is more than book knowledge or experience. Wisdom is the ability to make good decisions.

Did you know that this same offer is open to you? God wants to give you wisdom for your life. In fact, it's the one thing you can ask of God that He will give generously (James 1:5)

Are you overwhelmed by the choices you need to make? Are you nervous about the next season of your life? Are you scared you're going to mess everything up?

Get on your knees and pray. Ask God to give you wisdom.

What is
wisdom,
why do I **need** it,
and how do I **get** it?

BOTTOM LINE

God is ready and waiting to give you heaping doses of wisdom.

OWN IT

igniteyourfaith.com has a great article, "Top 10 Tips for Life."—based on wisdom from the book of Proverbs.

POWER PRAYER: *Dear God, I desperately want wisdom so I can live a life that honors You and serves others. Open up my heart and mind to Your wisdom.*

POWER PASSAGE

"Give your servant therefore an understanding mind to govern your people, that I may discern between good and evil, for who is able to govern this your great people?"

1 Kings 3:9

DAY 43

WHAT DO MOM AND DAD KNOW?

Why should I listen to my parents? They don't know anything. They live in another century. What do they know about my life?

You're about ready to bust out of the house and live on your own. The last thing you want to hear is another whiny lecture about listening to your parents.

Hear me out for a second. I know your parents probably do live in another century, and they might not totally understand you. Maybe they seem demanding. Fine. But have you ever stopped to consider that God may have given you those parents for a reason?

I don't know your situation. I don't know who your parents are. Chances are they are just trying their hardest to see that you don't make the same mistakes they've made. They really do want to see you succeed, probably even more than they succeeded.

There will be a time when you'll be completely on your own. That's coming sooner than you think. There will be no Mom and Dad to blame for your troubles. No Mom and Dad to make decisions for you.

Let me just tell you this. When you get a little older, you'll begin to realize that your parents weren't so backward after all. You'd be wise to at least listen and consider their advice.

I know I probably sound like a crusty old crank, but God wants you to love, respect, and honor your parents. They do know something about life.

Sometimes your
parents
make **sense** after all.

BOTTOM LINE

You'd be wise to consider the advice of your parents.

OWN IT

Look up Exodus 20:12; Deuteronomy 5:16; Ephesians 6:2. What do these passages say about your relationship with your parents?

POWER PRAYER: *Dear God, I don't always understand my parents and the decisions they make. Sometimes I feel like they are always on my case. But I know You've given them to me for a reason, so help me to honor and respect them.*

POWER PASSAGE

A wise son hears his father's instruction, but a scoffer does not listen to rebuke.

Proverbs 13:1

WISE GUYS, WISE GIRLS

I was about to make one of the dumbest decisions of my life. Only I didn't know it at the time, because I thought the bright red Jeep on the lot was the coolest car in the world.

What I didn't know was that the car might have been stolen, had been through a flood, and the odometer had been rolled back to look like it had 100,000 fewer miles.

I somehow summoned enough brainpower to call a guy who was a few years older than I was. He'd bought cars before. His first words? "Dan, don't buy that car. That sounds like a shady deal."

It's easy to get emotionally wrapped up in the choices we make just like I'd gotten emotionally caught up in owning a red Jeep. Sometimes you fall in love with something so hard that you just can't see straight. That's why it's good to talk to someone who has an objective point of view. The Bible says that the best choices are made with a group of counselors.

Who's in your group? It could be your youth pastor, your parents, an older sister or brother, maybe even a favorite teacher. These people are very important—they see things about your situation you may not see. Are you willing to listen and hear their advice?

Honestly, sometimes I've ignored advice from good people. It always comes with a big "I told you so," and a lot of regret. Don't make my mistake. And next time you're tempted to buy a too-good-to-be-true red Jeep, give me a call.

It's a good idea to get **advice** from other **godly people.**

POWER PASSAGE

Without counsel plans fail, but with many advisers they succeed.

Proverbs 15:22

BOTTOM LINE

Listening to the advice of multiple counselors saves heartache later.

OWN IT

Ask yourself today: *Who is in my circle? Who do I go to for advice and wisdom? Are they people who follow Christ?*

POWER PRAYER: *Dear God, thank You for the wise people You have put in my life. Help me to listen to their wise counsel and advice.*

DAY 45

TALK TO ME

I don't know what to do. For the last several months, Jenny had been agonizing over her immediate future. Should she graduate early from high school and take prep courses at the community college? Or should she graduate with the rest of the class? Should she go to college with her best friend or should she go where her sister went?

Each choice had good and bad aspects. Each choice was supported by her parents and close friends.

One Monday, after a weekend of wrestling and worrying left her anxious, she found a note in her locker. It was from her best friend. It simply said, "Have you prayed about your decision?" Jenny thought, *I have prayed a few times, but I guess I haven't gotten too serious about it.* So Jenny decided to stop asking people, stop talking about her decision, and just take a few days to pray over it.

Prayer is usually the last thing we do when making a tough decision. We might offer up a few bland prayers, but do we really get on our knees and get serious before the Lord?

Why don't we pray first? Maybe we don't pray because we think our decisions are too trivial for God. Or maybe we don't pray because we're afraid of God. But God wants to hear us. "Talk to me," He says.

I've been where Jenny was—several times in my life. Honestly, I really didn't know what exactly to pray, but I was able to muster the words, *God, show me.*

Maybe it's time for you to do that today. God wants to give you guidance about the difficult decisions in your life. All you have to do is ask.

God is
approachable
at every hour, for
every need,
in **every situation**
you face.

BOTTOM LINE

Prayer shouldn't be our last resort, but our first option.

OWN IT

Ask yourself: What is the best time for me to pray? How can I make sure that I pray to God every day?

POWER PRAYER: *Dear God, I need You. I cannot live one day without You. Thank You for hearing my prayers and being available all the time, 24/7.*

POWER PASSAGE

Call to me and

I will answer you,

and will tell you great

and hidden things that

you have not known.

Jeremiah 33:3

DAY 46

IT'S NOT JUST ANOTHER BOOK

It doesn't make any earthly sense. Here you are trying to decide which college to attend or who to date or what job to take and I'm telling you to take time in the Bible. How does a several-thousand-year-old book help you today? Right now, right here?

God's Word answers your questions, because His Word is not just any other book. It's alive. It's powerful. It's living. We don't read God's Word just to get another pithy answer or grab some inspiration for the day. A lot of other books can do that.

We read the Word because the Word reads us. It is God speaking to our hearts. It has the power to change us, to grow us, to move us closer to being the image of Christ.

That's why every series of choices must begin and end with the Bible. Make it a daily practice to read the Bible. You don't have to read six chapters a day. Maybe you just think on a single verse for 24 hours. Don't know where to start? Try Psalms or Proverbs or the Gospel of John.

You'll be amazed at how God can use one verse to change your perspective.

We don't **read the Word** just to "get answers." We read the Word because the **Word is alive** and speaks to us.

BOTTOM LINE

God speaks to our hearts through His Word.

OWN IT

To get started, check out my book, *Teen People of the Bible*. It's a 100–day devotional. Or check out my weekly devo, "Then & Now" on crosswalk.com.

POWER PRAYER: *Dear God, thank You for Your Word. Help me to read it and know that You're speaking to me. Help its power to touch my life every day.*

POWER PASSAGE

For the word of God is living and active, sharper than any two-edged sword, piercing to the division of soul and of spirit, of joints and of marrow, and discerning the thoughts and intentions of the heart.

Hebrews 4:12

DAY 47

GOD OF THE MAYBES

Jonathan was a young man of action who seized every opportunity to win victories for Israel and for God. So it was no surprise that he and an armor-bearer took out a whole platoon of Philistines. What is interesting is that Jonathan didn't wait for God to give him a 100 percent guaranteed assurance that his mission would be successful.

Jonathan's words to his armor-bearer before the battle include the word, *maybe*. "Maybe God wants us to do it. I'm not totally sure. But there is an opportunity here. Let's go for it."

That's real life. That's faith. You'll rarely have a burning-bush, lightning-in-the-sky moment where God tells you, "Do this" or "Do that." Life is a series of choices, opportunities, and open doors.

You have one life to live. You can spend it analyzing, wrestling, wondering. Or you can be like Jonathan—a person of action.

After you've weighed all the advice, prayed, listened to the Word, and sought advice, it's time to put one foot in front of the other and do something.

God doesn't want
  you paralyzed by fear.
He **empowers** you to
    make choices
and stick with them.

BOTTOM LINE

Real life and real faith consists of action and adventure.

OWN IT

Read Jonathan's story in 1 Samuel 14.

POWER PRAYER: *Dear God, help me to be bold like Jonathan. When I see a need, give me the courage and strength to meet that need.*

POWER PASSAGE

Jonathan said to the young man who carried his armor, "Come, let us go over to the garrison of these uncircumcised. It may be that the LORD will work for us, for nothing can hinder the LORD from saving by many or by few."

1 Samuel 14:6

DAY 48

JUST DO

In high school, my buddies and I took our favorite Nike slogan, "Just Do It," and shortened it to "Just Do." We decided we were going to live life on the edge. All out. Full throttle. No holding back.

Sometimes this attitude got us in trouble. Like when we took off without our parents in Belgium while on a church trip. They weren't too thrilled about that one! Or the time we locked a friend in a storage closet at camp.

But I think we were on to something big. We didn't want to live ordinary lives. We wanted to do something big for God. In his letter to the Philippians, Paul said, "Hey, you have heard me preach to you, you've read the Scriptures, now do them."

Notice that word *do*. It's simple but powerful. You only have one life to live. Do you want to spend it second-guessing, analyzing, and fretting? Or do you want to spend it actually doing something?

Many teens are afraid to trust God completely. They kind of hold back and wait for life to just happen to them. As if someone is going to tap them on the shoulder and hand them their future.

Doesn't happen that way, folks. As Nike said … as Paul said … you've got to just get out there and *do*.

You can live a life of **second-guessing** **or** you can live a life of **impact**. You can't live both.

BOTTOM LINE

Don't sit back and wait for life to happen to you. Just do.

OWN IT

Ask yourself this week: *What are some things I know I can do to make a difference, in my school, in my community, in my family? What are some obstacles holding me back?*

POWER PRAYER: *Dear God, help me to be a person of action and faith. I don't want my life to consist of waiting, wondering, and confusion. I want to make an impact on the people You've put in my world.*

LIFE, A SEASON AT A TIME

In Chicago, we have two seasons, winter and road construction. Or at least it seems that way. As soon as you grow tired of one season, the other one comes rolling in. (Unless winter stays too long like it did last year!)

Life is also full of seasons. I used to think that when I wore a gown and mortarboard and graduated high school, I had to choose right then and there what I would be doing for the next 50 years. I was so wrong.

I had dreams and goals and desires, but what I didn't realize was that life has seasons. Seasons of high school. Seasons of college. Seasons of singleness. Seasons of marriage. Seasons of one job, seasons of another job.

You don't have to have your entire life planned out like I thought when I was younger. It's not a bad idea to get your life plans on paper, but know that they will certainly change as circumstances and opportunities change. This is all part of God's plan for molding us, shaping us, and using us for His glory.

The best way to look at life is one season at a time, with an eye on the future. If you're in college, don't stress out about your career. If you're still in high school, don't fret about what fraternity to join in college.

Take life as it comes, a season at a time.

Do I have to have
my entire life
planned out,
or can I take it a
season at a time?

For everything

there is a season,

BOTTOM LINE

Life happens a season at a time, so
it's best to focus on what's in front
of you.

and a time for every

matter under heaven.

Ecclesiastes 3:1

OWN IT

Do a Bible search on the word *wait*.
To make it easier, try the free Bible
online at biblegateway.com.

POWER PRAYER: *Dear God, help me
to live life a season at a time. The
future can be so overwhelming, but
I trust that You have control of all of
it. Help me to rest in Your goodness.*

WHOSE LIFE IS IT ANYWAY?

I think it's very important to get advice from parents, pastors, and people you trust. They have experience and wisdom you don't have. But, don't kid yourself. The choices you make are up to you. Ultimately, it will be you standing before the Lord at the end of your life. It will be you answering for how you spent the time, talent, and resources He gave you.

Nobody else will stand there for you. So, don't let anyone else live your life for you. It's easy, as a teen, to follow whoever is most powerful—parents, friends, family, coaches, youth pastors, and other influences.

All of these people are important. They all have wisdom to share that can help shape the direction of your life. They all have a critical role to play in the person you are becoming.

But make no mistake. The choices you make have to be your choices. Wouldn't you hate to look back on your life and say, "I think God wanted me to be here, but I let someone else convince me to be here"?

Make sure your faith is really your faith. Make sure the direction you head is a direction God wants you to go.

Some may try to live their lives through you, but you have to remember that you own your choices. You're accountable to God for the life you live.

Don't let anyone
live your life
for **you.**

POWER PASSAGE
So then each of us
will give an account of
himself to God.
Romans 14:12

BOTTOM LINE
Advice is important, but ultimately you are accountable for your own choices.

OWN IT
Check out the book, *Making It Real: Whose Faith Is It Anyway?* by T. Suzanne Eller.

POWER PRAYER: *Dear God, I want to live my life for You. I want to live the life You intended me to live, not the life others think I should live. Please give me the wisdom to know the difference.*

WHO IS IN YOUR EAR?

Everyone tells you that you need to have good friends, because your friends determine who you are and where you go. That's true, but it's a little more complicated than that.

Sometimes you befriend people you're trying to help. Maybe their family life is dysfunctional, or they're struggling with issues. You don't want to abandon them. If you picked only perfect friends, you'd never be available to lift up those in need.

Jesus didn't exclude troubled people from His circle. In fact, He went out of His way to hang with the people everyone else rejected—sinners, tax cheats, lepers, thieves, drunkards, liars, murderers. He hung out with kind of a dangerous group.

What's important is who you follow, who you allow to influence your life. Are they friends who share your values, or are they friends who encourage you to violate what you know is right?

Sometimes you have to take a stand, even against people you love. Jesus did. He rejected advice from His own brothers (John 7:1–9). He corrected His closest friends (Matthew 16:23). He had to do this because He had to follow the will of God.

The influence of a friend is a powerful thing. Be careful who you listen to.

Are you
listening
to the
right people?

POWER PASSAGE

Do not be deceived:

"Bad company ruins

good morals."

1 Corinthians 15:33

BOTTOM LINE

Choose your friends wisely, because your friends influence you more powerfully than anyone else does.

OWN IT

Read what the Bible has to say about friendship. Check out these passages: Psalm 55:12–14; Proverbs 17:7; Proverbs 18:24; Proverbs 22:24–25; John 15:13–15; James 2:23.

POWER PRAYER: *Dear Jesus, I know that You are the greatest friend, because You laid your life down for me on the Cross. I want to be that kind of friend for others. Help me also to choose influencers who draw me closer to You.*

DAY 52

WHAT'S BEST FOR ME?

Angela had her choice of colleges to attend. She really wanted to go to a big state university. There was so much about it she enjoyed. But her father was dying and she needed to be close to him. So she chose a smaller college only a few hours away.

Some people might think, *that's not fair. Angela should do what she wants.* But Angela chose to put her father's needs above her own.

Most of our choices revolve around what is best for us. And the world is screaming, "Do what you want. Do what feels good." However, as a believer we're called to something higher.

We have Christ as our example. He put aside the comforts of heaven to come to earth, live as a man, and go to the Cross for our sins. He made the ultimate sacrifice. Without His sacrifice, you and I and everyone who believes in Him would be headed for an eternity without God.

So is it really asking that much for you and for me to consider the effect our choices have on the people God has called us to serve? Maybe we can put aside some of our desires so that others can succeed.

I'm glad Angela chose a college near her home. Not only did her sacrifice help her father in his last days, it enriched my life. You see, her journey that began at that smaller college took her on a path to Chicago, where she found me (or rather, I found her).

When you're making **choices**, remember that your choices affect **more than just you**.

BOTTOM LINE

When making choices, think of the people who will be most affected.

OWN IT

Read Jonathan's incredible story of sacrifice on pages 150–59 of *Teen People of the Bible*.

POWER PRAYER: *Dear God, develop in me an unselfish heart. Help me to see the ripple effects of my choices, so that I consider others as I pursue my dreams. Thank You for your sacrifice for me.*

POWER PASSAGE

Let each of you

look not only

to his own interests,

but also to the

interests of others.

Philippians 2:4

DAY 53

CHOOSING TO WORK

He walked up to me, hands folded across his chest, a scowl on his face. He was a cranky old guy who offered a lot of unsolicited advice. I knew I was in for another lecture. "You kids just don't know how to work hard like we did when we were kids." Ah, loved that one. Especially after three hours of basketball practice, which followed an entire day of working with my dad. Not to mention algebra homework and speech class. Nice.

I don't know if teens work less or more than they did 50 years ago, and I don't really care. But I do know that work is important, not just to cranky old guys, but to God.

A lot of people think work is punishment. Some Christians even think it's Adam and Eve's fault because they ate that forbidden fruit. Not true. It was God who instituted work. In fact, God Himself works. He worked to create the world. Jesus worked, spending long hours in Joseph's carpentry shop.

The world says hard work is to be avoided at all cost, but God says work is beautiful. He sees the fruit of our labors and is blessed. And one day He will look at our lives and examine what we did with our hands. Was it done well? Was it done for His glory?

Don't be afraid of hard work. Embrace it. As soon as you're old enough, find a job, even if it isn't your favorite place to work. And do it well. You'll be surprised at how good you feel and how much you learn about yourself.

Because work isn't just for the benefit of cranky old guys. Work is a gift from God.

Is **work** part of the **curse?**

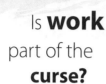

BOTTOM LINE

Work is a gift to be embraced, not a curse to be avoided.

OWN IT

Check out Jonathan Dodson's article, "How Should We Then Work" at boundless.org.

POWER PRAYER: *Dear God, thank You for the gift of work. Help me to approach every job as if this job is for You. Help me to work hard and do my very best, no matter the size or significance of the task. Give me strength and courage to work with integrity.*

POWER PASSAGE

Whatever your hand

finds to do,

do it with your might,

for there is no work or

thought or knowledge

or wisdom in Sheol,

to which you are going.

Ecclesiastes 9:10

THE THREE R'S

Responsibility. That was a word I heard more in my household than almost any other word. "Dan, you need to be responsible."

I'm sure you hear that word, too, don't you? It kind of sounds like the end of all things fun. But one thing I've discovered in the last few years is that a life of responsibility—and I dare say discipline—brings a life of freedom.

You see, nobody respects an irresponsible or lazy person. But those who are respectful, honest, and hardworking get more opportunities to succeed.

A life of doing what you want when you want sounds great. But after a while, it's empty and lonely. Nobody wants to hire a slacker. Lazy guys rarely get dates, at least with girls worth spending time with. And colleges usually don't graduate kids who fail to complete their required courses.

Start now on a life of discipline and maturity. It starts with little things, like taking care of your stuff, showing up on time for class, pitching in around the house. When you're old enough, find a job. You might even volunteer at church or a local shelter.

Why all the extra effort? Because the road to your dreams isn't paved with fool's gold, but hard work and yes . . . *responsibility*. Hmm, that word doesn't sound so bad after all.

The sooner you take **responsibility,** the sooner people will **respect** you.

BOTTOM LINE

Responsibility might not be the cool thing, but it's the fastest way to your God-given dreams.

OWN IT

Check out the cool blog, The Rebelution by Alex and Brett Harris (therebelution.com). Read their article, "I Won't Grow Up and You Can't Make Me."

POWER PRAYER: *Dear God, help me to avoid the temptation to pursue fun at the expense of growing up and pursuing Your plan for my life. Help me to act and live responsibly before You.*

POWER PASSAGE

For even when we were with you, we would give you this command: If anyone is not willing to work, let him not eat.

2 Thessalonians 3:10

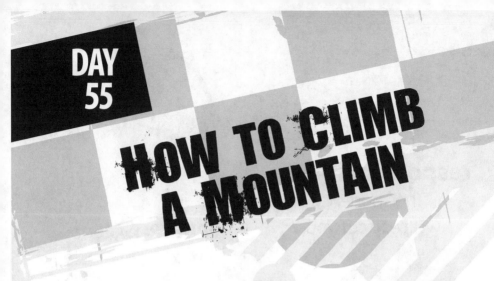

HOW TO CLIMB A MOUNTAIN

X $-Y$. H_2O. *Mass versus Volume.* Ahh, Tara's head was bubbling with math and equations and science. *If I have to redo this one more time, I'm going to explode. Why do I have to take this dumb class? Can't I just fast-forward through college?*

Tara knew what she wanted to be when she grew up. While the other girls talked about makeup and boys, she talked about airplanes. She was going to be a pilot. But why couldn't she just get there already?

What Tara didn't understand, at least at the moment, and what's often hard for us to understand, is that life is about finishing and completing small goals. We all want to fast-forward to the day we're piloting the airplane or cooking in the hotel kitchen as a chef or engineering a building project or leading the worship band. But we don't want to do the hard work that will get us to that point.

The question shouldn't be, *how can I find the easiest path to my dreams?* Instead, it should be, *am I doing the little things now that will help me learn what I need to know to get me to my goals?* The math that Tara hates may one day help her pilot a plane. The endless chord progressions might help a piano student turn into a professional musician. The early mornings at the pool might help the swimmer become an Olympian.

A day at a time. A class at a time. A practice at a time. Small goals that lead to a big life.

A **life of purpose**

isn't achieved all at once. It happens by accomplishing small tasks, **one day at a time**.

BOTTOM LINE

The unimportant tasks you face every day are important if you want to achieve your God-given goals.

OWN IT

Take a sheet a paper and write out some of your goals (get accepted into college, become a musician, make the varsity team). On the flip side write out some of the little things you can do today and every day to help you reach those goals.

POWER PRAYER: *Dear God, help me to be faithful every day in those little things, the routine, mundane tasks of life so that I fulfill Your desire for me.*

POWER PASSAGE

Therefore, since we are surrounded by so great a cloud of witnesses, let us also lay aside every weight, and sin which clings so closely, and let us run with endurance the race that is set before us.

Hebrews 12:1

DAY 56
THE BIG DATING QUESTION

Your heart skips a beat. Your hands are clammy and wet. Your forehead breaks out in beads of sweat.

There she is. She acts as if she likes you, but does she? Are you reading the signals wrong? The big question: should you ask her out?

So we're at Day 56 and we finally got to the big dating question. If you skipped ahead to this page, that's OK. I would have done the same thing.

But you're wondering, do I ask this girl out? Or if you're a girl, do I accept? What does God say about dating? How does a godly young man or woman get together with the person of their dreams?

There are a lot of books, a lot of advice, a lot of disagreement on what exactly is the "right" way to date. Every family and every situation is different.

Here are a few basics that everyone should heed. First, keep God at the center of any relationship. Second, put the feelings of the other person above your own. Third, submit to the accountability offered by your families and your local church, where godly men and women can help guide you.

Above all, resist the hookup culture where sex is easy and hearts are easily broken. Instead, embrace God's best in every relationship.

This might be the scariest time of your life. But it can also be the most wonderful.

What's the best way to find that **person** of **your dreams**?

BOTTOM LINE

Embracing God's best in pursuing a relationship isn't always easy, but it's always best.

OWN IT

Check out the book, *When God Writes Your Love Story* by Eric and Leslie Ludy.

POWER PRAYER: *Dear God, I want to honor You in all my relationships, but especially with that special someone. Help me to resist temptations and to wait humbly for Your leading. Above all, help me to show respect toward young people of the opposite sex.*

POWER PASSAGE

Keep your heart

with all vigilance,

for from it

flow the springs of life.

Proverbs 4:23

DAY 57

THE MYTH OF "THE ONE"

As long as we're talking about dating, can I knock down a popular Christian myth? It's the myth of "the one." It goes like this, "There is a Mr. or Mrs. Right out there, and you're bound to find them." Doesn't that sound wonderful?

Here's the problem. What if "the one" chooses to go out with someone else? Does that mean God messed up?

I don't think so. God's will is not some unhittable bull's-eye. As you walk with God and serve others, God will allow you to interact with like-minded people of the opposite sex. You'll have opportunities to get to know them and others with whom you share a spiritual and physical attraction.

So stop beating yourself up while looking for that perfect one. Relax, wait on the Lord, and trust that in His timing, He'll give you opportunities to meet a person you can love.

Why is it so **hard** to find **"the one"**?

POWER PASSAGE

"Do two walk together, unless they have agreed to meet?"

Amos 3:3

BOTTOM LINE

Instead of pursuing the perfect person, pursue God and serve others.

OWN IT

Ask yourself these questions: *Am I looking for qualities in a person that I am not willing to display in my own life? What am I doing to allow God to develop character in me that others might find attractive?*

POWER PRAYER: *Dear God. I want to know You and pursue You. Develop in me the character traits that will help me to become a godly person of character that can serve my future mate.*

THE PERFECT GUY

Donna opened her top drawer and pulled out a wrinkled sheet of notepaper. With tears, she read through the list of qualities she was looking for a in a guy. *Will this guy ever show up? Or maybe I'm just not attractive enough. God, I have tried to be a girl who honors You. I've stayed away from guys who wanted less than Your best.*

Donna's frustrations are common. If you're a Christian girl, you wonder where all the good guys went. Guys with high standards of purity. Guys with a passion for God. Guys who take life seriously.

Don't lose heart. And don't let the enemy tempt you to lower your sights. You want to experience love as God intended it to be, shared with someone whose soul is spiritually, emotionally, and physically knit to your own.

You'll never find Mr. Perfect. He doesn't live on your street. He doesn't take classes at your school. He doesn't attend your church. He doesn't exist.

But the desire God has put in your heart to spend life with a man who will cherish you, honor you, and love you as Christ loves His church is a natural desire. You're not out of line with His will, and you're not "boy crazy." Your longings are human and your desires are just.

So hang in there and strive to become that person, a young woman that every Christian young man desires, a woman after God's own heart.

Are there any **good guys or girls** out there, and what do they **look like?**

BOTTOM LINE

A girl's desire to love and be loved is a God-given desire.

OWN IT

Check out Jackie Kendall's book, *The Young Lady in Waiting.*

POWER PRAYER: *Dear God. You know the longings of my heart. You put in me a desire to love and be loved. I know that only Your love truly satisfies. Help me to wait patiently for a young man of God.*

POWER PASSAGE

The steps of a man

are established

by the LORD,

when he delights

in his way.

Psalm 37:23

DAY 59
IN PURSUIT OF THE PERFECT GIRL

All day, Cooper could barely concentrate. *That new girl at youth group last night was hot! And she talked to me. I can't believe it.*

Hot. Sometimes it seems like that's the only criterion guys use to evaluate a potential girlfriend. I know. I was a teenage guy too.

There's nothing wrong with hot. God wired men to be physically attracted to the opposite sex. But hot can't be your only measure.

Ask yourself these questions before you let your hormones explode. *Is she a believer? Is her love for God obvious? Does she carry herself with natural grace and beauty?*

Here are some even bigger questions to ask. *Are you a young man of God prepared to cherish and honor and respect a young woman of God? Are you willing to honor her boundaries and her parents' boundaries? Are you ready to serve and sacrifice and lead her in a way that draws her closer to Christ?*

I know. You're not really thinking these thoughts. Your friends may not be asking these questions. But if you wish to honor God with your relationships, with your love life, with your pursuit of a woman, these are questions you need to ask.

Cooper knows and you know that there has to be a lot more to a Christian girl than "hot."

How do I find a **girlfriend** who **honors God?**

BOTTOM LINE

A wise young man looks for a girl who radiates beauty on the inside and the outside.

OWN IT

Check out *Boy Meets Girl* by Joshua Harris.

POWER PRAYER: *Dear God, help me to pursue a girl who honors You with her life. Help me to be guided not just by my feelings and my attractions, but by Your Spirit. Give me the grace to honor and serve that special girl.*

POWER PASSAGE

An excellent [woman]

who can find?

She is far more

precious than jewels.

Proverbs 31:10

DAY 60

MONEY MATTERS

In high school, Mark rarely went out to eat with the rest of us. "I want to save my money," he said. We thought he was kind of weird. Why wouldn't he want to have a good time?

Well, when Mark paid cash for a brand-new car his senior year, I suddenly realized how smart he was. Unlike me—who had blown my hard-earned cash on restaurants, expensive clothes, shoes, and a bunch of other stuff that quickly lost its luster.

Like Mark, I worked a job in high school and had my own money. Unlike Mark, I was foolish and had very little to show for my efforts. It's a lesson I had to learn the hard way.

If you have a job and earn your own money, that's a great start. But be wise with your money. Be a saver. And when you have the opportunity, be generous toward God's work and the needs of others.

Jesus said that the way you handle money is a good barometer of your heart. So start now by working hard, saving your money, and giving where you can.

Your friends might laugh at you now, but when you're picking them up in a brand-new car, who will be laughing then?

If it's your **money**, why can't you **spend** it the way you **want?**

POWER PASSAGE

"For where your treasure is, there will your heart be also."

Luke 12:34

BOTTOM LINE

Learn early how to handle money and you'll avoid the pitfalls that ensnare so many people.

OWN IT

Ask your mom or your dad or a youth pastor to help you set up a budget for the money you earn. It doesn't have to be complicated, just a simple paper chart with fields for *giving, saving, fun money,* and other categories.

POWER PRAYER: *Dear God, help me to be wise with my money. I realize that all that I have is a gift from You. I want to use it wisely.*

SECTION THREE

DIRECTION—
What Should I Do with My Life?

Talk About It
(with your friends, your parents, or your pastor)

> What are some of the toughest choices I'm facing right now, and who am I asking for advice?
>
> What are my gifts? What are the things I enjoy doing?
>
> What passions has God put in my heart?
>
> Am I pursuing purity in my relationships?

Go Deeper
Here are a few resources to help you investigate the ideas we talked about for the last 20 days.

Web sites:
setapartgirl.com
sloppynoodle.com
igniteyourfaith.com
christiancollegeguide.net

Books:
When God Writes Your Love Story
    —Eric and Leslie Ludy
I Kissed Dating Goodbye—Joshua Harris
Lady in Waiting—Jackie Kendall
Teen Devotional Bible—Zondervan

Magazines
YW (Youthwalk Devo by Walk Through the
    Bible—http://www.walkthru.org/site/News
    2?page=NewsArticle&id=5383)
Susie Magazine—susiemagazine.com
EC (Essential Connection) Magazine—LifeWay

SECTION FOUR

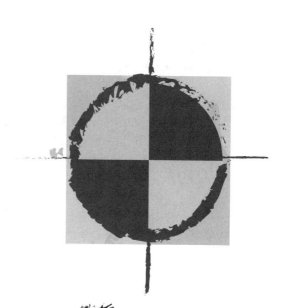

DEVOTION —
STAYING TRUE IN A WORLD OF LIES

DAY 61

WHOSE FAITH IS IT ANYWAY?

When King Nebuchadnezzar conquered Judah, he captured thousands of young Jewish teens. These guys were ripped from their home and forced to live in Babylon. Babylon was a radically different place than Judah so it challenged everything they had known about God.

For instance, the Jewish law had specific requirements for their diet. But now the king pressured them to violate the law. And it seems most teens went along with the king. Except Daniel and his three buddies, who stood alone.

Imagine the pressure they faced from thousands of their fellow Jewish teens. *C'mon, guys; our parents aren't around. We're on our own. Loosen up!*

Ahh, the pressure to give in, to cave on your values. You know what that's like, don't you? Or maybe you don't. But whether you go off to a state university or a Christian college, whether you're flipping burgers or running errands for the company president, your day in Babylon will come. A time, a moment, that season of life when your mom and dad and youth pastor aren't around to tell you how to think and live.

The question will be, will you cave like the thousands of nameless Jewish teens perhaps did or will you rise up and hold fast to your faith like Daniel and his three buddies?

In other words, is your faith just a hand-me-down from Mom and Dad or is it something you own?

Is **my faith** **my own** or is it **passed down** from Mom and Dad?

BOTTOM LINE

Sooner or later you'll have to decide what *you* believe.

OWN IT

Daniel was a young man who made a profound difference in Babylon. Read his story in Daniel chapters 1, 2, 4, and 6.

POWER PRAYER: *Dear Jesus, help me to develop a bulletproof faith that withstands the pressure to compromise. I want to know what I believe so I can defend it and share it.*

POWER PASSAGE

But Daniel resolved that he would not defile himself with the king's food, or with the wine that he drank. Therefore he asked the chief of the eunuchs to allow him not to defile himself.

Daniel 1:8

DAY 62

THE BLESSING OF BOUNDARIES

It was my last day on the job and a co-worker was treating me to lunch at a Chinese restaurant. While I hung up my jacket, he ordered drinks for both of us. When the waiter brought them to the table, I thought, *OK, this looks interesting. Maybe its Chinese root beer. I love to try new stuff. And I love root beer.*

Only it wasn't root beer. I didn't find that out until my nose caught a whiff of the drink just as my lips touched the bottle. In that nanosecond, a single stray thought weaved its way through my mind. *What's one drink, man? What kind of weirdo are you going to be, anyway?*

But then I remembered my parent's stories of alcoholism in the family. I recalled the verses in Proverbs that warn of alcohol's dangers (Proverbs 20:1; 23:31).

I sheepishly set the bottle down and mumbled, "Uh, can I get something else? I really don't drink."

It was an awkward moment, but I found the courage, because years before I had set boundary markers for my life. I wasn't about to violate them over a forgettable lunch.

Where are your boundary markers? Sooner or later, you'll be tested as I was. It may be a dorm room, the backseat of a car, or a friend's house.

Your parents, your youth pastor, your older siblings won't be around to tell you what to do. You're going to have to fall back on the beliefs you've internalized—those values that you know to be true and right.

Are **boundaries** that **important** in life?

But Daniel resolved that he would not defile himself with the king's food, or with the wine that he drank. Therefore he asked the chief of the eunuchs to allow him not to defile himself.

Daniel 1:8

BOTTOM LINE

Decide now where your boundaries are—and determine to keep them there the rest of your life.

OWN IT

Reflect on Daniel 1:8.

- *Take inventory of* your value system. Have you purposed in your own heart those things you will not do?

- *Write* these down as personal pledge to follow God's Word. Share them with a friend who can hold you accountable.

- *Pray* for God's strength in living inside your boundaries.

POWER PRAYER: *Using your personal pledge, write a prayer about the boundaries God wants you to set and pray for His strength to do so.*

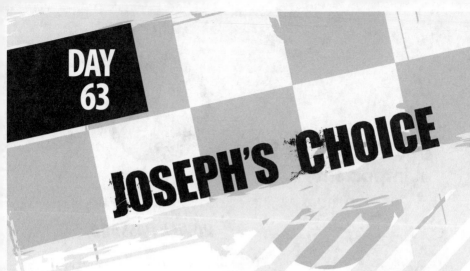

JOSEPH'S CHOICE

E very day she shot Joseph that seductive look. Every day she dressed a little more provocatively. Every day she tried to lure Joseph into a sexual relationship.

Joseph was away from his family. He could be free to celebrate sexual expression. His parents wouldn't know. His Jewish friends wouldn't know. But God would know. That meant everything to Joseph.

If I were writing the story, I'd say, "And Joseph did the right thing and lived happily ever after." But God wrote Joseph's story. Joseph's obedience cost him everything—his job, his reputation, his freedom.

Here's a shocker. Doing the right thing may cost you something. It may cost you friends. It may cost you family. It may cost you a job.

But in the end, it always pays to do the right thing. God didn't forget Joseph, and later it was this young man's character that led him to become the prime minister of the world's most powerful country.

If you live to please people, you'll end up making the wrong choices, but if you live to please God, who sees all, then in that moment of temptation, you'll have the courage to walk away.

Joseph's
faith in God
helped him keep his
purity when it
was **tested**
the most.

BOTTOM LINE

It's better to please God, who sees everything, than to please others who don't have your best interests at heart.

OWN IT

Read Joseph's story in Genesis 39.

POWER PRAYER: *God, give me the courage and strength to resist temptation, to follow You in every way. Even if it costs me something.*

POWER PASSAGE

He is not greater

in this house than I am,

nor has he kept back

anything from me

except yourself,

because you are his wife.

How then can I do this

great wickedness

and sin against God?

Genesis 39:9

DAY 64

IS TEMPTATION WRONG?

I s temptation wrong? Those ugly thoughts that crawl onto the threshold of our brain, lustful thoughts, bitterness, criticism, anger. Are those sinful? You might think so, but consider this. Jesus Christ, the Perfect God-man, was tempted.

Yes, you read that right. Jesus spent 40 agonizing days in the wilderness with Satan himself, whose desire was to get the Son of God to sin. But Jesus didn't give in to temptation, even in the slightest form, proving that He was God, and therefore, incapable of sinning.

Jesus also endured temptation to show us that temptation, in and of itself, isn't sin. Temptation becomes sin only when we act on it. When thoughts turn to actions (James 1:15).

We live in a sinful, fallen, wicked world. We can limit our exposure to temptation, but we can't escape it. So we'd better have a game plan to resist its power.

What was Jesus's response to each temptation? He used God's Word to fight the enemy. And so should you. Next time "the tempter" wants to get you in his grip, dig into your Bible, and let God's Word give you the answers you need.

You will be tempted every day, often multiple times a day. But only with God's strength can you resist and avoid the traps of sin.

How could
Jesus Christ,
the Son of God,
the **Perfect Man**,
be **tempted**?

BOTTOM LINE

Temptation is only sin when we act on it.

OWN IT

Memorize these power verses for times of temptation: James 1:13–15; Romans 6:23; Numbers 32:23; Galatians 6:7.

POWER PRAYER: *Dear God, please give me the strength in the day of temptation. I know sin can have a devastating effect on me, on my relationships, on my entire life.*

POWER PASSAGE

Then Jesus said to him,

"Be gone, Satan!

For it is written,

"'You shall worship

the Lord your God

and him only

shall you serve.'"

Matthew 4:10

DAY 65

THE MONSTER INSIDE

When you read the words of Romans 7:10–25, you might think they were the words of some really bad sinner, some guy who just didn't have his act together.

Would you believe they are the words of Paul, maybe the greatest Christian who ever lived? Paul wrote honestly about the struggle inside, the struggle with sin.

This is the great secret most Christians don't discuss. We go to church, put on a cheesy smile, carry our Bible a certain way, and act as if everything is fine.

If you were to be completely honest, and if I were to be completely honest, we, like Paul, would amid that we struggle with sins.

The truth is, even though you are a believer, you still have that old nature inside. The Bible calls it "the old man" or "the flesh." This guy loves to sin.

But here's the good news. Our weakness is God's strength. He is right there in our hardest struggle and wants to help us through each day, every day, in every temptation.

If I'm a **Christian**, why do I still **struggle** with **sin**?

BOTTOM LINE

Every Christian, everywhere, struggles every single day with sin. Only Jesus can help us win that struggle.

OWN IT

Take a sheet of paper and write down your deepest struggles with sin. Keep this list in your Bible and pull it out often and pray over each one, asking God for victory.

POWER PRAYER: *Dear God, please, be there in my struggle. I need You every hour of every day to help me live apart from sin.*

DAY 66

GOD INSIDE

How many times have your parents or your pastor said to you, "If God was sitting right here in this room, would you do that?"

Did you know that if you're a believer, God actually is right there with you? Yes, that's right. He's inside of you; you are in the presence of the Holy Spirit. This is why the struggle against sin that you and I face every day is winnable.

Paul, who knew a little something about sin and temptation, said that the only way to get victory over sin is to let the Spirit lead our lives. What does that mean? Well, it means we obey that still small voice prompting us. It means we immerse ourselves in God's Word. It means we submit our will to the will of God. It means we ask God's help every time we're tempted to sin.

You see, in every situation, we have a choice. We can yield to that monster inside, the flesh that wants us to sin. Or we can yield to the Holy Spirit, who empowers us to do right.

Walking with God isn't just about saying no to sin. It's about embracing our best friend, the Holy Spirit who lives inside and wants to see us become more like Jesus Christ.

How do we **win** the daily **struggle** against **sin**?

POWER PASSAGE
But I say,
walk by the Spirit,
and you will not
gratify the desires
of the flesh.
Galatians 5:16

BOTTOM LINE

We win the battle of sin when we embrace the Holy Spirit's presence in our lives.

OWN IT

Every temptation has an equal and opposite opportunity to serve God. Take out that sheet of paper where you listed your toughest sin battles. Now next to each one, write a prayer, asking God to give you something He would have you do instead, like complimenting the person you're jealous of, forgive the person who wronged you, send an encouraging email to the one who seems to dismiss you.

POWER PRAYER: *Dear God, I want to yield to Your Holy Spirit within me. I want to live the life You want for me. Help me to resist the enemy and his temptations.*

DAY 67

DON'T FEED THE BEAST

N ever, ever feed a black bear." I was given this warning every year as I arrived at summer camp, in the backwoods of northern Minnesota. The reason we didn't feed black bears was because their stomachs were much larger than any snacks we had in our backpacks. When the snacks ran out, they'd go after us. I didn't feed the bears because I didn't want to be their next meal.

Every one of us has a beast inside. A beast the Bible calls our flesh. Just like the black bears, if we feed that beast, it will want more. The monster inside is never satisfied with a snack. He will demand more and more of *you* until he has eaten away at your soul. So Paul gives us some common-sense advice in Romans. He says, *"make no provision for the flesh."*

What feeds the beast? It's different for everyone, but I've got a few ideas. How about TV shows that promote sex and drug use? How about friends who brag about the trouble they get into? How about Web sites that gratify desires you know need to be starved?

Only you know your biggest sin struggle. So if you are really serious about winning this struggle, every day, do yourself a favor. Don't feed the beast.

What are some ways I can **limit** my **exposure** to **tempting situations**?

BOTTOM LINE

Feeding the beast only makes the beast stronger.

OWN IT

Pull out that list of struggles again. Next to each one, write friends, TV shows, music, movies, books that encourage you to sin. Now read Matthew 5:30 and ask the Lord to help you decide which influences to eliminate from your life.

POWER PRAYER: *Dear God, please give me the courage to eliminate influences that influence me to sin. Help me to have discernment about situations and friends and people so that I can more fully walk with You.*

POWER PASSAGE

But put on the Lord Jesus Christ, and make no provision for the flesh, to gratify its desires.

Romans 13:14

DON'T FEED SOMEONE ELSE'S BEAST

D o you want to know the biggest myth in the universe? It's this: *what I do has no effect on anyone but me.*

The truth is that every person has a circle of influence. That circle might only be five people wide. It might be 5 million people wide. But every one influences at least one person, usually more, with the way he or she lives.

So you have to ask yourself, *am I helping or hurting someone's walk with God?*

Girls, are you helping the guys in your life in their battle with lust? Are you dressing in a way that promotes pure thoughts? As a guy, let me just share how tough this battle with lust is. We constantly have to guard our eyes so they don't wander and usher in a flood of tempting thoughts.

Guys, are you treating the girls in your life with dignity and respect? Are you leading them along in your relationships, or are you honestly pursuing godliness so they know where they stand? Are you pushing them to do go farther physically?

The Bible encourages us to consider others. That means we don't just live our lives as if in a vacuum. No, we examine our actions and ask ourselves, *How am I helping the faith of my brothers and sisters in the Lord?*

Do my **activities** **help or hurt** someone else's **walk with God**?

POWER PASSAGE

And let us consider

how to stir up

one another to love

and good works.

Hebrews 10:24

BOTTOM LINE

God calls us to examine our lives so that the way we live helps others draw closer to God.

OWN IT

For advice and tips on modesty and purity, check out www.pure freedom.org.

POWER PRAYER: *Dear God, help me to live in a way that builds up the faith of others. If there are areas of my life that I'm unintentionally hurting someone's walk, please show them to me so I can change. I don't want to keep someone from experiencing Your blessings.*

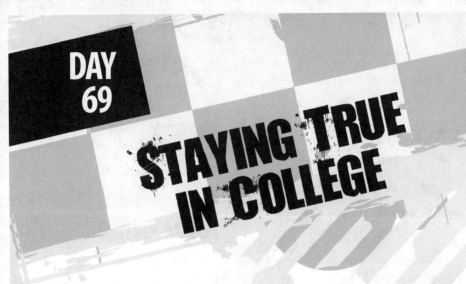

STAYING TRUE IN COLLEGE

S o your bags are packed and loaded in your family's car. You've checked your list like 17 times. On the way to school, you think of that new life ahead of you.

You've heard the warnings. You've talked to your pastor and youth pastor. Your parents are ready with more. "Hold on to your faith," they all say.

Inside you're thinking, *I'll be fine. I'm strong. I've grown up in church. I don't plan to abandon everything I know.* Still, you're worried a little bit. *What if there aren't any other Christians on campus? What if my teachers are all atheists?*

Well, I want to say to you that it is possible to keep your faith, but you need a plan. Here are a few tips.

- Find a good Bible-believing and preaching church and get immediately plugged in. You might even ask to speak to the singles or college pastor and ask him to help keep you accountable.

- Find a Christian campus group such as Campus Crusade for Christ or InterVarsity Fellowship.

- Ask your parents to send you good resources like Christian magazines and books.

- Give your cell phone number to your home pastor or youth pastor and ask him to call you from time to time to check up on you.

Is it possible to **hold onto my faith** in **college**?

BOTTOM LINE
Plan ahead to stay true to your faith in college.

OWN IT
For more great tips on keeping your faith in college, check out J. Budziszewski's excellent book, *How to Stay Christian in College.*

POWER PRAYER: *Dear God, I want to stay true to You in school. Help me find good friends and influences that can keep me accountable. I want to redeem these years for You so I can make a difference in the world.*

POWER PASSAGE

Blessed is the man

who walks not

in the counsel

of the wicked,

nor stands in

the way of sinners,

nor sits in the seat

of scoffers.

Psalm 1:1

NEXT-LEVEL DEVOS: GO TO CAMP

E very summer the list arrived in the mail. Every year the list was longer. Every year there were those favorite things I couldn't bring to summer camp:

- **No Sony Walkman**
  (those lame portable tape players everyone had 15 years ago.)
- **No magazines**
- **No boom box**
  (the slightly less portable radio/tape players everyone had 15 years ago)
- **No video games** *(Yes, we had those back then.)*
- **No books**

What were we allowed to bring? Bibles, notebooks (we usually lost the first day), bug spray that smelled bad but didn't work, flashlights that got one usage out of them, and ugly shorts Mom bought at K-mart.

So you're thinking, how in the world did you make it without your music, your video games, your gadgets that keep you wired?

Do you want the honest truth? The quiet wasn't so bad. In fact, unplugging from everything that so easily distracts helped me focus on what was really important—my relationship with God.

I don't know if you do camp. Maybe the idea of sleeping on the ground gives you the shivers (literally, on cold nights). Maybe walking a mile to the shower isn't your thing. Maybe dirt and sand and water make your skin crawl.

That's fine, but you can still unplug from the noise of the world and get alone with God. You can listen to His gentle voice upon your soul.

To **hear God** speak,
sometimes
you need to
unplug, **unwind**,
and have some
quiet time alone.

I think we don't allow quiet time because we are afraid of what God might communicate.

Take some time to unplug and unwind and take in the voice of your heavenly Father.

BOTTOM LINE

Turn up the quiet. Find rest in God.

OWN IT

- Walk or run outside (without your iPod).
- Turn down the car stereo and just spend time in prayer (please don't close your eyes).
- Try getting up a little earlier every morning. Spend even 15 minutes alone with God before the rest of the family gets up.

POWER PRAYER: *Dear God, I want to hear You. I want to think about You, in those quiet, still moments. Help me to clear the clutter of life away.*

POWER PASSAGE

"Be still, and know that I am God. I will be exalted among the nations, I will be exalted in the earth!"

Psalm 46:10

DAY 71

NEXT-LEVEL DEVOS: CHEW ON IT

When I hear the word *meditation*, I think of moms who do yoga, Buddhist monks who aren't allowed to speak, and a weird neighbor who once claimed to communicate with Elvis.

So if the word *meditation* spooks you, I understand.

But there is a meditation that helps us to know and understand God in a powerful way. And it's not as scary as it sounds. It's simply taking the words of God, spelled out in the Scripture, and chewing— mentally—on them for a while.

It just might supercharge your Bible reading. Instead of speed-reading through ten chapters, you might take one or two or three verses and roll them around in your head.

And you don't just leave those verses in your Bible. You bury them in your brain, carrying them with you to school, to work, and when you go out with your friends.

You'll be surprised at how quickly the Bible turns from a dusty book on your shelf to a book that's alive and filled with fresh inspiration and instruction for every area of life.

Does an old, dusty, **outdated book** have anything to say to **my life?**

BOTTOM LINE

Biblical meditation transforms your Bible reading into an experience that changes your life.

OWN IT

Take some time today to read Psalm 1. Ask yourself these questions. *What are the benefits of thinking deeply about God's Word? How can I change my Bible reading habits so I get more out of it?*

POWER PRAYER: *Dear God, the words You speak to me through the Bible are not ordinary words. They are full of power and life. Apply them to my heart so that I change and become more like You.*

POWER PASSAGE

But his delight

is in the law

of the LORD,

and on his law

he meditates

day and night.

Psalm 1:2

NEXT-LEVEL DEVOS: BURY IT

Think. What would you do for $250? Maybe you shouldn't answer that. But do you want to know what I did once?

I memorized the entire Book of Galatians. I was in college, I was going on a trip to Israel, and I desperately needed the cash. So I memorized an entire book.

But even though I had ulterior motives, memorizing Galatians lasted me far longer than the measly cash. In fact, to this day, there are times I'm struggling and the verses from Galatians cascade to the front of my brain.

If meditation takes your time with God to the next level, memorization blasts it into outer space. How? Your mind is a like a computer hard drive. The Word of God stays there and the Holy Spirit brings it to mind exactly when you need it.

So I encourage you to memorize Scripture. Memorize as much as you can. Not because I'm going to give you $250. But because God will give you much more than that. His living Word inside your heart.

You're mind is like a hard drive. If you **fill it** with **God's Word**, it will **stay there** for the exact moment you will **need it**.

BOTTOM LINE

Memorizing Scripture takes God's Word and permanently implants it in your life.

OWN IT

OK, try memorizing today's power passage. Here's a clue, start a word or a phrase at a time and build from there. Who knows? Maybe you'll be able to memorize an entire chapter.

POWER PRAYER: *Dear God, I want to store Your Word in my heart. Give my mind clarity so I can implant Your truths in my life.*

POWER PASSAGE

I have stored up your word in my heart, that I might not sin against you.

Psalm 119:11

NEXT-LEVEL DEVOS: HOW TO UNDERSTAND THE BIBLE

What keeps you from reading the Bible every day? Maybe it seems confusing or maybe every time you open it, you end up in Leviticus or with a list of funny-sounding names.

OK, maybe it's time to look at *how* you read your Bible so you can start hearing God speak to you—getting the most out of His Word.

Everyone approaches the Word a little differently, so I won't say there is a one-size-fits-all approach, but here are a few tips to get you started:

- Begin in a book like John, which really sums up what Jesus's mission on Earth was.

- Find a good study Bible. At the end of this section, I'll list several helpful Bibles for teens.

- Find a good devotional book. I'm biased, but you might check out *Teen People of the Bible*

- Journal. Write down your thoughts and feelings and what you feel God might be saying to you at the moment.

- Listen to some hymns or worship music while you read. Music is a powerful tool that can prepare your heart to hear God.

The most important part of your daily time in God's Word is prayer. Begin every day asking God to open your mind and hear to hear what He wants to say to you today.

With a little digging, you can find **great treasures** in your daily **Bible study**.

BOTTOM LINE

Reading the Bible doesn't have to be boring or difficult.

OWN IT

For more helpful tips, check out the article, "8 Ways to Know Your Bible" at igniteyourfaith.com.

POWER PRAYER: *Dear God, open up my mind. Speak to me through Your Word. Help me to apply its truths to those corners of my heart You wish to claim as Your own.*

NEXT-LEVEL PRAYER: HONEST TO GOD

B rett grew up in a religious house. Every week he went to church and heard long, memorized, recited prayers. But when Brett put his faith in Christ, he saw other believers praying to God as if God was their best friend. *Wow, is that possible?*

Prayer doesn't have to be hard. Prayer doesn't have to be long. Prayer doesn't have to contain fancy religious words. In fact, those kinds of prayers are not really what God is looking for.

To pray is really to be honest with God. If you read David's prayers in Psalms, you'll find that David opened up his heart. He told God exactly what was on his mind. He poured out his struggles and asked for help.

If God is our best friend, then why not just be real and honest with Him?

Whether this is your first time to pray or you've been praying since you were in diapers, it's time to dispense with the formality and big words and just start talking to the Lord, who wants to hear from you.

Why do we
hold back our
deepest thoughts
from the
only One
who understands?

BOTTOM LINE

Be real and honest with God—that's what He's waiting for.

OWN IT

Read the rest of Psalm 77 and read David's heartfelt prayers. You might also check out Habakkuk 1 and Job 23.

POWER PRAYER: *Dear God, I don't always know what to pray or how to pray. But I do know that I should pray. I may not always say the right words, but You know my heart. I want to know You. Thank You for listening and understanding.*

NEXT-LEVEL PRAYER: TRUE CONFESSIONS

Whoever first said, "confession is good for the soul," was wise, because confession is the first step toward a relationship with God that goes to the next level.

Let's face it, we all mess up. Every single day we sin. Sin forms an uneasy barrier between us and God. Since Christ has already forgiven all our sins, all we have to do to recharge our relationship with God is to confess our sins.

You might say, "Doesn't God already know my sins?" Yes He does. But God wants us to admit them as well. When we confess them, we agree with God about our sinful condition. Confession is much more than just admitting our sins, it's a willingness to seek God's help in changing our ways.

Our quiet time with the Lord reveals those deep, dark sins in our hearts. It is that hidden sin that keeps us from experiencing God more fully.

The reason God takes our sin so seriously is because it hinders the enjoyable relationship between us and Him. God is a holy God, who can't allow sin in His presence. So if we desire to know Him more fully, we'll bow before God, humble ourselves, and acknowledge our sinfulness.

Then God restores us to fellowship, cleansing us from sin and renewing our relationship.

Sin breaks our
healthy relationship
with God, but
confession
restores it.

POWER PASSAGE

If we confess our sins,

he is faithful and just

to forgive us our sins

and to cleanse us

from all

unrighteousness.

1 John 1:9

BOTTOM LINE

Confession of sin breaks down the walls between God and us.

OWN IT

For more on what the Bible says about confession and hidden sin, check out Psalm 32:5; Proverbs 28:13; and Psalm 51.

POWER PRAYER: *Today, write out your own prayer of confession, agreeing with what He has revealed to you from reading these Scriptures.*

DAY 76

NEXT-LEVEL PRAYER: ADORATION

On Day 74, we talked about God being our best friend and how we can tell Him anything. That's still true, but sometimes we can get so casual with God that we show Him no respect.

Part of prayer is telling God our problems. Part of it is praying for others. Part of it is confession of sins, and today we're going to see that another part of prayer is adoration.

Adoration seems like a big, huge, heavy Bible word. It is. It simply means to worship. Did you know that God desires our worship?

I think this is the part of prayer we miss the most. We're busy people, sending up huge laundry lists of things we need. But before we ask Him for a good grade in English, for a boyfriend on the basketball team, for a new car for graduation, and acceptance into college, we should first bow down in humble worship.

If you think worship is something you can only do in church or when listening to your favorite music, think again. Worship is something we do every time we bow before our heavenly Father and express how wonderful, how mighty, how holy He is, and how undeserving we are of His love. True worship is simply recognizing God for Who He is.

God isn't a buddy.
He isn't "the Man upstairs." He is the **holy**, righteous **God of the Universe**.

BOTTOM LINE

Prayertime should always begin with true worship of God.

OWN IT

A great way to enhance your worship is to look up the names of God in a Bible dictionary (such as the *Holman Illustrated Bible Dictionary*). They may even be listed in the back of your Bible.

POWER PRAYER: *Dear God, fill my heart with worship of who You are. I want to bow my heart's knees in prayer and surrender to Your majesty and Your power. You are awesome and holy and all-powerful.*

POWER PASSAGE

I bow down toward your holy temple and give thanks to your name for your steadfast love and your faithfulness, for you have exalted above all things your name and your word.

Psalm 138:2

WHY YOU NEED CHURCH

The alarm clock goes off and you hit the snooze. After playing in a Saturday night baseball game, all you want to do is get some sleep. Then your Mom knocks on the door. Her strangely chipper voice jolts you out of unconsciousness, "Time to get up for church."

What is the big deal? Do we have to go to church? Can't I sleep in? All they do is sing and listen to some boring guy tell stories for an hour.

You drag your tired body up, sleepwalk into the shower, and get ready for Sunday.

A lot of people are asking the question these days, "Is church really that important?" You can listen to sermons online. You can watch church on TV or the Internet. So why go to a local church?

Well, for one thing, church is where God meets with His people (Matthew 18:20). You see, God didn't create us to live alone; He created us to live out our faith in community with other believers. Believers who aren't perfect and have their own struggles, but who can encourage us to walk with God.

Church is where you hear God's Word. It's where you find comfort from other Christians. It's where you seek accountability, helping you stay away from trouble.

Don't disparage church. Make church a priority, both while you're at home with your parents and when you move away to college.

Besides, you really won't miss that extra hour of sleep anyway.

Is going to

church

really

that important?

POWER PASSAGE

And let us consider

how to stir up

one another to love

and good works,

not neglecting

to meet together,

as is the habit of some,

but encouraging

one another,

and all the more

as you see the

Day drawing near.

Hebrews 10:24–25

BOTTOM LINE

Church is where God interacts with you and me and gives us the tools we need to live out our faith.

OWN IT

Check out the question, "Why Is Church Attendance Important?" on gotquestions.org.

POWER PRAYER: *Dear Jesus, I know the church is important to You. I know being part of a church means being part of a worldwide movement. I know that You died for the church. Help my attitude for the church. Help me to be faithful to the church.*

HUMILITY: THE KEY TO GREATNESS

It was my first year of college and somehow I got roped into a skiing trip with the singles group at my church. Not having skied before, everyone told me it would be easy. Those same people told me to "just go down the advanced hill and you'll get the hang of it." Great idea, if you enjoy hurtling down a mountain at breakneck speed, falling halfway thru, and rolling like a giant boulder before slamming into a group of girls at the bottom of the hill.

The entire rest of the day was an exercise in humility. But looking back, I know God allowed things like this to show me that I wasn't as cool or as great as I thought I was.

Believe it or not, the Bible says humility is the doorway to greatness (Matthew 19:30). All of us are born with a dose of pride. And God says that until we allow Him to knock that out of us, He can't use us in the way He desires.

What is humility? It is a foot-dragging woe-is-me attitude? Is it letting everyone step all over you? No, humility is simply putting others needs, thoughts, concerns over yours.

In fact, the Bible says that God actually resists—or fights against—the proud (1 Peter 5:5). But He gives grace to the humble. So we have a choice to make in life. We can have God fighting for us or have God fighting against us. I know which one I want.

What is **humility**?

Does it mean that I allow everyone to **walk all over** my life?

BOTTOM LINE

Humility is God's way of using you for His kingdom.

OWN IT

For an in-depth look at humility, check out *Humility, True Greatness*, by C. J. Mahaney.

POWER PRAYER: *Dear God, thank You for allowing humbling experiences in my life to show me that I'm simply a sinner undeserving of Your grace, but wrapped in Your love. I can't do anything effective in this life without You.*

POWER PASSAGE

This is the one to whom I will look: he who is humble and contrite in spirit.

Isaiah 66:2

HOW TO KEEP YOUR PURITY

You turn on the TV; it's there. You go to the mall; it's there. You pop in your favorite movie; it's there.

Sex. How does a Christian obey God, live a life of purity, and save sex as a gift for a future husband or wife? Is it even possible? How is it possible?

Most people would say no. But remember that God would not ask you to do anything that His grace can't empower you to do. The only way you will stay pure is to have an action plan:

1 Realize sex is a wonderful gift created by God, as an expression of love between a husband and wife. God created sex.

2 Determine that you refuse to open that gift until you can present it to your future mate on your wedding night.

3 Understand that you as a human are weak and can only do this in the power of the Holy Spirit.

4 Know that you must not put yourself in a dangerous position where you'll be tempted to shortcut God's plan for your sexual life.

5 Realize that saving yourself for marriage and living a life of purity is a sacrifice you're giving back to God as a gift to Him.

Is it possible to keep your **purity** in a world bombarded with **sexual messages**?

BOTTOM LINE

Sex is good; it was created by God and to be expressed only in marriage.

OWN IT

For a powerful in-depth Bible study on this subject, check out the *Great Love* Bible study series by Chandra Peele. (discovergreat love.com)

POWER PRAYER: *Dear God, give me the strength and courage I need to stay pure until marriage. I want to give my future spouse a gift of purity to be unwrapped by Your design on our wedding night. Help me stay strong.*

POWER PASSAGE

I appeal to you therefore, brothers, by the mercies of God, to present your bodies as a living sacrifice, holy and acceptable to God, which is your spiritual worship.

Romans 12:1

WATCH YOUR EYES

I'm about to reveal something that will shock you, so I hope you're sitting down.

Ready?

OK, when I grew up, we didn't have a TV in our house. I can hear you already. *Wow, how did you survive?* Back then, my parents felt that television would not be a good influence in our home.

And honestly, I didn't really miss much. I did really weird things like read books, listen to the radio, and ride my bike. I know, strange, but somehow I made it.

As I look back, I realize that my parents gave me a gift. They limited the amount of entertainment I consumed. They protected me from much of the garbage of the world. As a parent and father and pastor now, I'm eternally grateful that they loved me enough to guard my heart and mind and soul.

I don't know what you're restrictions are. Maybe your parents are stricter than a Marine sergeant, or maybe they have no rules. But let me ask you this. What are your personal entertainment boundaries?

I'm not here to say you should throw your TV out. I'm not going to give you a list of "acceptable" music and movies. But I'm asking you to be aware of the power of media. Music has a way of sticking in your head. Movies tend to set the standard on a lot of things like kissing, sex, romance, and fashion. Inappropriate images and conversations online can lead you into risky behaviors.

So let me ask you: What's on your ipod right now? What TV shows do you watch? What books make up your library? What Web sites do you frequent?

Does it **matter** what **movies** I watch or what **music** I listen to?

I ask because I know that what you put into your mind will come out in your life.

BOTTOM LINE

Media is more powerful than we realize. We must create sensible boundaries.

OWN IT

For great movie, music, and entertainment reviews, check out the Web site, pluggedinonline.com.

POWER PRAYER: *Dear God, give me discernment and wisdom about the choices I make. Help me to filter wisely what I allow into my life so I can more effectively serve You.*

POWER PASSAGE

I will not set before my eyes anything that is worthless. I hate the work of those who fall away; it shall not cling to me.

Psalm 101:3

SECTION FOUR

DEVOTION—
Staying True in a World of Lies

Talk About It
(with your friends, your parents, or your pastor)

Daniel set boundaries for his life—way before he was tested. What are some of your boundaries? What are things you absolutely won't do despite the pressure from people around you?

What motivated Joseph to resist the advances of his boss's wife? What keeps you from doing the wrong thing when nobody is looking?

Everyone is tempted. Is temptation itself wrong? When does it become sin?

What is the monster inside? How can a Christian control the monster? How can you starve the monster—and the monster inside your friends?

Go Deeper
Here are a few resources to help you investigate the ideas we talked about for the last 20 days.

Web sites:
susiemagazine.com   purefreedom.org
igniteyourfaith.com   pluggedinonline.com

Books:
How to Stay Christian in College—J. Budziszewski
Holman Illustrated Bible Dictionary
Stop Dating the Church—Joshua Harris
Humility: True Greatness—C J. Mahaney
Great Love (for Guys)—Chandra Peele
Great Love (for Girls)—Chandra Peele
Cherished—Chandra Peele
Secret Keeper—Dannah Gresh
The Bare Bones Bible Handbook for Teens—Jim George

Study Bibles:
Extreme Teen Study Bible—Thomas Nelson
Student Life Application Bible—Tyndale House

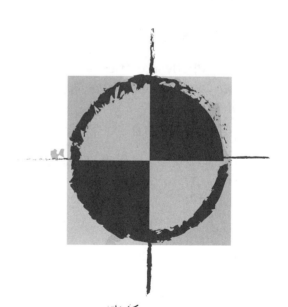

DELIGHT—
FINDING JOY IN A HARD WORLD

RIPPED FROM HOME

You're ripped from your house in the middle of the night. You barely have time to grab your wallet, keys, iPod, and phone. You toss a few clothes in a bag, grab a can of soup from the kitchen, and you're in the van. As you roll through your neighborhood one last time, you pass familiar haunts—school, the mall, church—and mentally wave good-bye.

Rewind this story eight centuries and you find Daniel and thousands of his closest Jewish friends. Kidnapped from their homeland. Dumped into a foreign country. Forced to learn a new language. Everything they ever knew was about to change. Big time.

Nobody likes being moved, uprooted, pushed from his or her comfort zone. However, God often uses change to shape our character.

What keeps you sane in the middle of sudden change? Your faith in God. It's is the only sure thing in a crazy world.

So if your world is upside down, now is the time to lock in on God. Crack open your Bible, take a walk and pray, and find some good Christian friends to lean on.

Eventually, you can look back and see how God weaved the separate strands of your life into a compelling story sure to shape your character and bring Him glory.

How do we
handle the
sudden changes
in our lives?

Then the king commanded

Ashpenaz, his chief eunuch,

to bring some of the people

of Israel, both of the royal

family and of the nobility,

youths without blemish,

of good appearance and

skillful in all wisdom,

endowed with knowledge,

understanding learning, and

competent to stand in the

king's palace, and to teach

them the literature and

language of the Chaldeans.

Daniel 1:3–4

BOTTOM LINE

God allows change to mold our character and to force us to depend on Him and Him alone.

OWN IT

Reflect on Hebrews 6:19; Hebrews 13:15; Deuteronomy 31:6.

- *Anchor* yourself in God's promise to stay by your side.

- *Recognize* your opportunity grow in fresh new ways.

POWER PRAYER: *Dear God, I don't know what to make of my new surroundings. I don't really like change too much. But I know this is for Your ultimate glory in my life. Help me to depend on You and to trust You with every new season of life.*

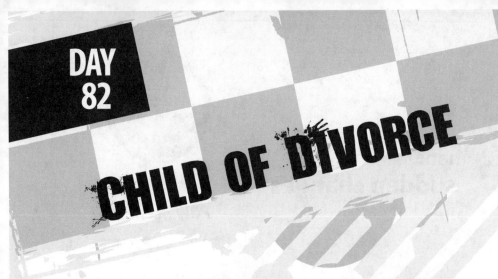

CHILD OF DIVORCE

Sydney sat on her bed, tears streaking down her face. She was crushed. *Why can't Mom and Dad put aside their selfishness and just stay together? Don't they care about me?*

During the summer of her junior year, her parents had sat her down and told her the news. They were going ahead with a divorce. They were doing this, they said, for her. They just wanted what was best.

This divorce had hit Sydney in unexpected ways. She had see it coming for a few months now and thought she was ready. But she wasn't ready. She was terrified.

Would she have to move? Would she lose her friends? What would happen to her younger brother and sister?

What should Sydney do? How should she react? And why would God allow this to happen to her?

There's a good chance that many who read this devotional have experienced the effects of divorce. What's tough is that nobody asked your opinion. Did you want your family to split up? Were you excited about shuttling between homes on Christmas and Thanksgiving? Were you thrilled about serving as a go-between, absorbing insults from both sides.

Here's some good news about divorce. God can redeem your dysfunctional family situation. Out of your pain, your brokenness, your experiences, God can mold you into something special in your generation.

It was that way for Sydney. As a youth leader, she now reaches out with compassion to confused children of divorce. She has

Why did God allow **my parents** to **split** up?

allowed God to use her difficult life circumstances for His ultimate glory.

BOTTOM LINE

God can use your parents' break-up for His glory in your life.

OWN IT

Check out Tim Baker's book, *Broken: Making Sense of Life After Your Parents' Divorce*.

POWER PRAYER: *Dear God, I know that You sovereignly chose my family and my background. It was no accident. It wasn't a slip-up on your part. Therefore, I praise You, and I want to take my pain and use it as a ministry to others.*

DAY 83

LOSING SOMEONE YOU LOVE

It has been barely a month since my good friend, Ben Kottwitz, passed away. Cancer took Ben from us early. He was only 34 years old and left behind a wife and two little kids.

There are so many things about Ben's death I didn't understand. Why did God allow his wife to live without the love of her life? Why did God allow these children to grow up without their daddy? Why did God allow a good friend to die?

I could give you a really good list of spiritual answers. But the truth is that I honestly don't know why God took Ben. But this one truth I do know. God hears our cries (Psalm 6:8). God weeps when we weep. When Jesus lost His best friend, Lazarus, He openly cried (John 11:35).

Will you ever get over losing a loved one? I don't think so. I think the scar that remains is our heart's way of helping us remember that person. But over time, it does get better.

A loss is made more acceptable when we know that the person we loved is in the arms of Jesus. My friend Ben is now with His Savior. He is basking in the glow of heaven. One day, he'll be reunited with his wife and his children. And eternity will wipe away the pain of death here on earth.

Why does God allow **people** we love **to die**?

BOTTOM LINE

We may not understand why God allows loved ones to die, but we know that He shares our grief.

OWN IT

Remember key truths when it comes to losing someone:

- *God is always in control, and His timing is perfect.* (Isaiah 55:9)
- *Jesus is the Resurrection and the life—those who know Him will go to Heaven.* (John 11:25)
- *Everything God allows is for our good.* (Romans 8:28)
- *The Lord hears your tears.* (Psalm 6:8)
- *God is with you in the midst of your loss.* (Isaiah 43:2)

POWER PRAYER: *Dear God, I don't understand why You take people away from us. But I do know that You're in charge and You are here with me. Stay by me. Hold me. Protect me.*

POWER PASSAGE

But we do not want you to be uninformed, brothers, about those who are asleep, that you may not grieve as others do who have no hope.

1 Thessalonians 4:13

DAY 84

FORGIVING SOMEONE YOU HATE

All my life, *forgiveness* was just another warm sounding Christian word. Until someone I loved hurt me so deeply. They took my words and my kind gestures and ripped a hole in my heart so big that even today I struggle to discuss it.

At first, I was angry. I wanted this person to be destroyed. But then the words of Ephesians 4:31–32 came cascading from the recesses of my memory. This time they were fresh.

It was as if Jesus was saying to me, "Dan, you've been hurt deeply, but I'm calling you to forgive." So I began the process of forgiving. It began in my own heart, where I slowly released the burden of bitterness and left it at the feet of Jesus. It didn't mean I suddenly wanted this person to be my best friend. But my thoughts slowly became less angry and more thoughtful and caring.

Why forgive? Most importantly, we forgive because Jesus has forgiven us. Stop and think about it. Our sins against Jesus are more outrageous than the worst sins anyone has ever committed against us. I think of specific sins I've committed against God, and I think of His grace toward me.

We forgive because it releases us from the bondage of bitterness.

We forgive because forgiveness is the only way to experience fully God's forgiveness in our own lives.

But I warn you. Forgiveness isn't easy. Forgiveness isn't instant. Forgiveness doesn't mean everything is suddenly fine.

It's messy. It's hard. It's repetitive.

Some days the thoughts of anger and revenge come rolling in, and we have to stop and forgive many times a day.

How can I possibly
forgive someone
who has
hurt me
so deeply?

Only God can help us forgive. Only God can give us the power to pass someone's faults from our own heart to the heart of God.

Are you struggling today with forgiveness? Lean on Him, the ultimate Forgiver.

BOTTOM LINE

We must forgive because Jesus forgave us.

OWN IT

If you really want to dig into forgiveness, I'd recommend one of two powerful books: *Choosing Forgiveness* by Nancy Leigh DeMoss and *The Healing Power of Forgiveness* by Ray Pritchard.

POWER PRAYER: *Dear God, the weight of bitterness is so heavy. Its darkness threatens to overtake my soul. Please give me the power to forgive, because You forgave me. Help me to live free of anger and free of bitterness.*

POWER PASSAGE

Let all bitterness and wrath and anger and clamor and slander be put away from you, along with all malice. Be kind to one another, tenderhearted, forgiving one another, as God in Christ forgave you.

Ephesians 4:31–32

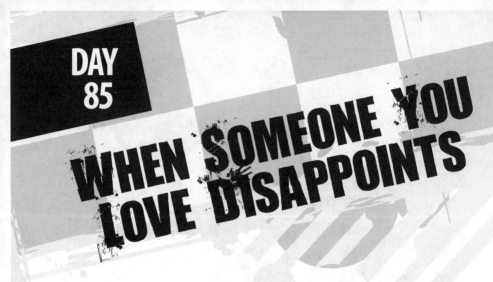

WHEN SOMEONE YOU LOVE DISAPPOINTS

One day he was a fixture at the palace, performing music and befriending the king's son. The next day, he was a fugitive from that same king, who was now gunning for David's head. One day he enjoyed friendship with a man he admired and respected. The next day he was fleeing a deranged lunatic who was bitterly jealous of David's accomplishments.

I'm guessing you've never known any kings. But you've probably had someone you respected bring you great disappointment. A youth pastor who walks away from the faith. A relative who suddenly turns on you. A friend who gets in trouble.

You worshipped the ground they walked on. You hung on their every word. You modeled their life choices. Then you see a side you wish you'd never seen. The sinful side. The prideful side. The evil side.

I've been there, and I know how it feels. Why does the disappointment run so deep? It's simple. Naturally, we want people we can look up to—role models, leaders, examples. But we set ourselves up for big-time disappointment because we put way too much faith in *people*. We elevate them so highly, they can only fall. That's not fair to them, and it's not fair to us.

Does that mean we should never trust anybody again? No. Does that mean we should be cynical and disrespectful to authority figures? No. What it does mean is that we should have a more balanced view of the sinfulness of man, even the greatest human beings God allows into our lives.

And ultimately, our faith should not be in *people*, however gifted or godly. Our faith should be in the Lord. David learned this lesson.

What do you do when **someone** you respect **lets you down**?

In Psalm 146:3 he says, *"put not your trust in princes."*

Has someone you respected disappointed you recently? Take this opportunity to renew your faith in God, who will never, ever fail you.

BOTTOM LINE

People will invariably fail, but God never fails.

OWN IT

Read the ultimate story of disappointment and betrayal, the story of Judas Iscariot in Matthew 26. Notice what Jesus called His betrayer in verse 50. He called him, "Friend."

POWER PRAYER: *Dear God, I know I should trust You always, but it's hard not to be disappointed when people I respect let me down. Help me to forgive them and to realize that they are sinners in need of the same Savior I need.*

POWER PASSAGE

Put not your trust

in princes,

in a son of man,

in whom there is

no salvation.

Psalm 146:3

THE GOD OF YOUR NIGHTMARES

T he storm will pass, let's stay out here." Probably the dumbest words I'd ever spoken. I was fishing with friends in Florida on the Caloosahatchee River. Storm clouds appeared on the horizon, but like good fishermen, we brushed them off and kept fishing.

The clouds didn't pass. They opened up and dumped hard, pelting rain. Waves rocked the boat, and we gunned it home.

The Sea of Galilee is known for its fierce storms. One time John and Peter and Matthew and the rest of the disciples were in a boat, and suddenly the sea whipped up a doozy of a storm. It was so fierce Matthew described it as a *tempest* or an *earthquake*. And remember, these fishermen were used to big storms. But this beat them all.

But in the midst of their fear, they forgot one thing. Jesus was in their boat. Jesus wasn't just an old sailor; He was the Creator. He made the sea and could still the waves.

Maybe you're in a storm today. Maybe you feel like the sea of life is going to overwhelm you in its waves. Maybe you're scared for your life.

Know this. If that same Jesus is in our boat, then you have nothing to fear. You might go through storms. You might face circumstances that rock your world. God doesn't promise a smooth-sailing journey through life.

But what He did 2,000 years ago, He can do today. He is the God of the storm and can get you safely to the other side.

Where is God
when
it hurts?

BOTTOM LINE

With Jesus in your boat, you have no need to fear.

OWN IT

Check out the story of the disciples' harrowing night on the sea in Matthew 8:24–27. In the margins of your Bible, near this passage, write in your top three fears.

POWER PRAYER: *Dear God, I'm facing a storm like I've never faced before. I'm scared, and I don't really know what is going to happen. I'm in need of You in my life. Please take my fear and turn it into peace.*

POWER PASSAGE

And behold, there arose a great storm on the sea, so that the boat was being swamped by the waves; but he was asleep. And they went and woke him, saying, "Save us, Lord; we are perishing." And he said to them, "Why are you afraid, O you of little faith?" Then he rose and rebuked the winds and the sea, and there was a great calm.

Matthew 8:24–26

FROM EVIL TO GOD

He was kidnapped by his own brothers, beaten up, thrown in a well, and almost killed. He was sold into slavery, forced to work for a boss whose wife tried to seduce him, and then thrown in prison on false rape charges. When he finally had his ticket out of jail, the man who should have defended him dropped the ball and forgot Joseph.

And that was all before Joseph was 30. Nice life, huh?

That's a lifetime full of injustices. Circumstance so completely unfair, so completely wrong.

But God allowed this evil to happen so that Joseph would be in position to save the world from starvation. God put Joseph through the meat-grinder so that he'd be physically, spiritually, and mentally ready to save the world from mass starvation as the prime minister of the world's largest country.

So when Joseph met face to face with his brothers, he was able to utter these words, "What you meant for evil, God meant for good."

What we don't see is that God is in control even of the evil in our lives. He allows it to happen, working it around for our good and for His glory.

What evil are you experiencing today, this week, this year? What injustice are you enduring? I can't tell you how, but I do know this. God is going to take that evil and turn it into good.

You see, people can do whatever they want to you, but they can't destroy you, because even the bad things they plot are used by God for your ultimate good. What a powerful promise of God.

How do we **make sense** of the **evil** in the world?

BOTTOM LINE

Every injustice is used by God to bring about good.

OWN IT

Discover powerful lessons from Joseph's life in my book, *Teen People of the Bible*.

POWER PRAYER: *Dear God, it's hard to understand why You allow evil. But it is comforting to know that the evil that people cause is used to bring about good in our lives and in others. Help me to trust You and better understand Your ways.*

POWER PASSAGE

As for you, you meant evil against me, but God meant it for good, to bring it about that many people should be kept alive, as they are today.

Genesis 50:20

DAY 88

WHY BITTERNESS BITES

Nobody travels with more stuff than the Darling family. Even when we travel overnight, my wife seems to pack for three weeks. With superhuman skill, we manage to cram it all into our minivan.

It's not fun to travel with excess baggage. You have to stuff it in the overhead compartment. You have to cram into a too-small car trunk. You have to lug it around the mall.

Bitterness is life's excess baggage. And yet we like to carry it around, bring it with us into new relationships. Instead of releasing our baggage and embracing forgiveness, we continue slinging it over our shoulders. We talk about our injustices whenever we get the chance.

But here's the thing about bitterness. It doesn't hurt our intended victim; it only hurts us. It distracts us from our main purpose. It destroys friendships. It weighs down our souls.

Jesus wants to take our baggage. He wants us to release the pain and anger of injustice. He wants us to throw it off onto Him so we can be free to live the life He promised.

What baggage are you lugging today? Ask God to take your bitterness and help you move on in freedom.

Why does
bitterness
always end up
hurting me
the most?

BOTTOM LINE

Bitterness never hurts its intended victim; it hurts the one who bears it.

OWN IT

The Bible says bitterness:

Destroys others—Ephesians 4:31

Hurts relationships—Colossians 3:19

Destroys us from the inside
    —Hebrews 12:15

It is a tool of the enemy
    —James 3:14, 15

*Has an effect on our physical
    bodies*—Psalm 32:3;
    Proverbs 15:30; 17:22; 14:30; 12:4

Keeps us from loving God fully
    —1 John 4:20

POWER PRAYER: *Dear God, I don't want to carry the baggage of bitterness. I want to release it to You. I know you're the God of forgiveness. I want to experience true freedom.*

DAY 89

IF I COULD ONLY

If you watch enough TV, you'll start to think that the secret to happiness is getting everything you want. Hamburger ads say you can "have it your way." Beer companies brag about the "high life" where everyone is happy all the time—with a beer in their hand.

But if that were true, then there would be more stories of people getting what they want—and ending up happy. Instead, we find the opposite. Almost every day the headlines are filled with another pro athlete, another actor or actress, another musician in trouble.

The real truth is that the glamour life is really not glamorous at all. If anyone proved that, it was Samson. He was given everything he wanted in life. He had the body everyone envied. He had the girl everyone wanted. He had the gifts everyone coveted. And yet Samson ended his life broken, blind, and as a captive to his enemies.

Today you might be thinking, *if my parents would only give me what I want, I'd be happy.* But think again. Maybe your parents want you to be happy, which is why they *don't* give you everything you want.

How do you deal with not getting what you want? You can pout and whine, or you can embrace your life as gift of God, knowing that everything the Heavenly Father sends or doesn't send your way is for your ultimate good. And remember, happiness doesn't come in a plastic package. It can't be slapped on the VISA or ordered online. Real happiness comes from knowing and experiencing God.

What would happen
if I got
everything
I wanted?

Every good gift and

every perfect gift

is from above,

coming down from the

Father of lights with

whom there is

no variation or shadow

due to change.

James 1:17

BOTTOM LINE

Getting what we want is not always the best thing for us.

OWN IT

Read Samson's epic tale of lost opportunity, tragedy, and grace in Judges 13–16.

POWER PRAYER: *Dear God, there are many things I think I need. There are many things I want, that I think will make me happy. But You know better. Please only give me what is good for me. I worship You as the great giver of good things, the Creator God. I know You withhold nothing good from my hand.*

A WORD FOR THE BROKEN

Nobody had more potential than Samson. Nobody wasted more talent. He was the poster boy for all that can go wrong in a life. Today he'd be the subject of ridicule on every late-night talk show.

But what's interesting is that just when everyone thought God was done with Samson, when the strongest man on the earth was reduced to a blind laughingstock in the prison of his enemy, God reached down and used this broken man to win one last great victory for Israel.

If you think God doesn't use broken, sinful, damaged people, think again. In fact, those are the very sort of people He chooses.

Can God still use you after you've given yourself away sexually? Can you be a vessel of honor after you've had an abortion? Can you come back to God even after you've run the other way for so many years?

The resounding answer is always yes. Why? Because you have a Savior, Jesus, who hung on the Cross to provide a way for you, me, and everyone who believes in Him to be whole again. The brokenness of His body bought our freedom.

So if you've messed up, if you have weaknesses, if you've looked in the mirror and discovered that you're not perfect, watch out. Because you're just the kind of broken person God really, really wants to use.

How much do I have to **mess up** before God **gives up on me?**

Then Samson called to the LORD, and said, "O Lord GOD, please remember me and please strengthen me only this once, O God, that I may be avenged on the Philistines for my two eyes."

Judges 16:28

BOTTOM LINE

Nobody is too broken and outside the reach of God's grace.

OWN IT

Check out the story of John Newton, a human slave trader-turned-preacher in the powerful movie *Amazing Grace*.

POWER PRAYER: *Dear God, I'm ashamed by my past. The enemy tries to remind me of my failures. But I know the scars of my sins cannot keep me from pursuing Your will in the future. Thank You for being my Savior, for giving me a second chance.*

LIFE AFTER THE BREAKUP

The telltale signs are there. He starts acting weird. She stops returning your calls. He ignores you in class. Then your gut starts to churn. Something's wrong.

Soon you're listening to a tear-stained confession. "I just want to be friends." *Just friends? C'mon, after all we've been through?*

Breakups stink, don't they? Everyone's patting you on the back. *It will work out OK. God has someone better. You didn't deserve this.*

But it doesn't ease the pain. You feel rejected, stupid, worthless. Nothing prepares you for the feeling of rejection.

Here's something to chew on. You have a Friend who understands rejection. Jesus was rejected by His own people (John 1:11). He was rejected by His closest followers (Matthew 26:75). He was rejected by the very people He came to save (Isaiah 53:3).

It is in this time of pain that you have a choice. Everything in you wants to be bitter, to lash out, to paint your ex-girlfriend or ex-boyfriend as an uncaring jerk. You can do that.

Or you can take your troubles to the Lord and know that He loves you and will never reject you. You can begin the process of healing, of hope, and yes, forgiveness. How did Jesus treat the people who rejected him? He sacrificed Himself for them, even as they taunted Him. He loved them. That should kick any desires for revenge or gossip out the window.

And one day you'll look back on this moment as a moment you realized that Jesus is the best friend of the rejected and the lonely.

Why does **life** seem so **worthless** after a major **breakup?**

BOTTOM LINE

Breaking up isn't easy, but there is a Friend who understands.

OWN IT

Check out the article "I Ate My Love Letter" by Jeremy Smith on deeperdevotion.com.

POWER PRAYER: *Dear God, I was not really ready for rejection. Those feelings I had are still there, and I'm not sure what to do with them. Please draw close to me, and help me move forward effectively in my life.*

POWER PASSAGE

The LORD is near to the brokenhearted and saves the crushed in spirit.

Psalm 34:18

WHEN LIFE ISN'T FAIR

I was standing on a dirt road in the middle of an Indian village when I heard a shuffling to my left. I turned my head to see a young boy scooting along the ground. He had no legs, but wore the biggest smile. I learned that he was a Christian who had never known what it was to walk, who lost his legs to a disease that in America was curable. He was proud of his faith in Jesus Christ and told me, in broken English, what a blessing it was to serve his Lord.

That's just one of many images I'll remember from my trip to India. It made me realize that no matter how bad life gets here in the US, no matter what God allows me to endure, somebody, somewhere, is worse off than me.

How do we get our eyes off ourselves? How do we stop dwelling on the little injustices in life? It's simple. Begin by finding somebody worse off than you and digging in to help their needs.

The truth is, life is not fair. But what's not fair is that most of us get to live in America, have access to health care and school systems and friends and food. Most of the rest of the world goes to bed hungry, with no shoes, and little to call their own.

Take time today to count your blessings and pray for those around the world who are less fortunate than you are.

Why does **life** have to be so **unfair?**

BOTTOM LINE

We stop thinking about the injustices of life when with compassion we dwell on those who are less fortunate.

OWN IT

Check out the Web site: kidsofcourage.com. It shares powerful stories of teens who are being persecuted for their faith around the world.

POWER PRAYER: *Dear God, thank You for giving us your complete, written Word. I know it is You, speaking to me. I want to treasure Your words and sew them into the fabric of my heart.*

POWER PASSAGE

As for you, you meant evil against me, but God meant it for good, to bring it about that many people should be kept alive, as they are today. So do not fear; I will provide for you and your little ones." Thus he comforted them and spoke kindly to them.

Genesis 50:21–21

IT'S JUST STUFF

They were the hottest thing on the market. Air Jordans by Nike. And every single one of my friends had a pair. Well at least it seemed that way.

But Mom said they were too expensive and that she'd buy me basketball shoes, Nikes even, but no Air Jordans. No matter how much I whined and complained and pouted, Mom wasn't giving in.

Then one day, I stumbled across these words in Philippians. *"Not that I was ever in need, for I have learned how to be content with whatever I have. I know how to live on almost nothing or with everything. I have learned the secret of living in every situation, whether it is with a full stomach or empty, with plenty or little"* (Philippians 4:11–12 NLT).

Wow, did I feel like a loser. Paul was content while confined for two years, and I was complaining about not having Air Jordans. Then I began to think of the images I had just seen at church, images of children in third-world countries. Some have never owned a single pair of shoes. They were just happy to have a handful of rice to sustain them through the day.

There is nothing wrong with having stuff. There's nothing wrong with looking forward to a new pair of shoes, of dreaming of the latest iPod or a new car. Where desire gets dangerous is when it consumes us. As an old man once told me, "Its OK to have stuff, just don't let stuff have you."

Why is it dangerous? Because stuff is just stuff. It fades, cracks, peels, stops working, and falls out of fashion. Stuff can't buy happiness. Only God brings happiness.

Why does it seem like we **never** have **enough stuff**?

BOTTOM LINE

Contentment is the choice to be happy with your own stuff.

OWN IT

Take this quick "heart check" when it comes to your stuff:

1. Do you ever find yourself saying, "If I could only have _____ _____, I'd be happy."
2. How much of your thoughts does this occupy? Has it kept you from thinking about God and about your important relationships?
3. What dishonest things have you been tempted to do to get your hands on that one thing?

POWER PRAYER: *Dear God, help me to be content with Your blessings. I know that I have in my possession so much more than I deserve. I thank You for Your bountiful blessings.*

POWER PASSAGE

"Keep your life free from love of money, and be content with what you have, for he has said, "I will never leave you nor forsake you."

Hebrews 13:5

UNEXPECTED FRIENDS

All through high school, Mike was my nemesis. We competed in everything, from the last starting position on the basketball team to the state essay-writing competition. But most of all, we competed for the affections of the same girl. Jesse had both of our hearts twisted in a knot.

My last two years in school were consumed by one desire: to one-up Mike. Instead of enjoying the ride, having a good time with friends, and deepening my relationship with God, I was a one-man wrecking crew with Mike as my only target.

Then one day, after we both graduated high school, I saw Mike in a stairwell at my old school. In that moment, the years of anger, competition, and jealousy melded into one profound feeling of regret. Perhaps I was maturing in my relationship with God, or maybe it was the look of pain I sensed in Mike's expression. Either way, my heart was heavy with the weight of my own sin. So I reached my hand out and said to Mike, "Dude, I'm so sorry for being such a jerk all those years. Will you forgive me?"

Interestingly, Mike and I have become great friends since. We discovered that, after all the hatred was removed, we had a lot in common. It is a friendship I could have enjoyed all throughout high school, had I not been blinded by my selfish rage.

You see what bitterness does? Bitterness destroys friendship, hurts relationships, and drives us to do things we really don't want to do. But mercy, God's mercy, removes bitterness and helps us love those we struggled to love.

Why do we show mercy? Not because people deserve it, but because God has shown us mercy when we *didn't* deserve it.

What's the point
of showing
mercy to those who
don't deserve it?

Is there a Mike in your life today? Someone you absolutely can't stand? Don't waste your high-school years with hatred. Seek mercy and you might find an unexpected friendship waiting.

BOTTOM LINE

Mercy heals and restores; bitterness blinds and destroys.

OWN IT

Take time and look at the word, *mercy* as used in the Bible. You might use a Strong's Concordance or even a Greek Lexicon (your church media library should have one). Or you can use the online tools at biblestudytools.com.

POWER PRAYER: *Dear God, I don't want to be consumed by hatred and bitterness. It destroys what You've created. Help me show mercy to others. You've shown me mercy.*

POWER PASSAGE

"Blessed
are the merciful,
for they shall
receive mercy."

Matthew 5:7

DAY 95

THE SECRET TO HAPPINESS

Let's be honest. The teenage years are some of the toughest years of your life. Not only is your body changing, but you are also having to deal with a lot of other junk. Friends who stab you in the back, relationships that unexpectedly break up, acne, term papers, overbearing parents, and probably 12 other pressures nobody understands.

You try talking to Mom or Dad but they really don't get you. Your youth pastor is funny and has a lot of good things to say, but you're embarrassed to share with him your deepest darkest secrets. And your siblings—well, maybe they're part of the problem!

OK, maybe these people really don't get you, maybe nobody does. But can I share something golden? God understands you. God will listen to you. And the truth is that He *is* the secret to a life of happiness.

But you say, *Dan, I've heard all that in Sunday School. It sounds nice, but it really doesn't work for me.* Well, maybe it hasn't worked, because you don't really understand real joy.

True joy doesn't come from our circumstances. Because sometimes life hands us a set of problems we didn't ask for. True joy comes from pursuing Christ relentlessly. Paul said that the person who knows Christ can be contented all the time, even when his world is upside down. And Paul would know, since he spent much of his ministry in cells, imprisoned for sharing the gospel.

Joy begins with a choice. You can allow your circumstances to weigh you down and cloud your view of God. Or you can release them into God's mighty hands, trusting that He is in charge of your world.

Why can't I ever seem to be **happy**?

POWER PASSAGE

Rejoice in the Lord

always;

again I will say,

Rejoice.

Philippians 4:4

Then God gives you a joy that endures whatever life brings.

BOTTOM LINE

Happiness isn't about what happens to you. It's a choice you make.

OWN IT

Check out the book *No Matter What, You Can Rejoice* by Michelle Glover.

POWER PRAYER: *Dear God, I want to experience Your deep, real, lifelong joy. Help me to look above my circumstances, to stop trying to find happiness in what happens to me. I want to have Your joy.*

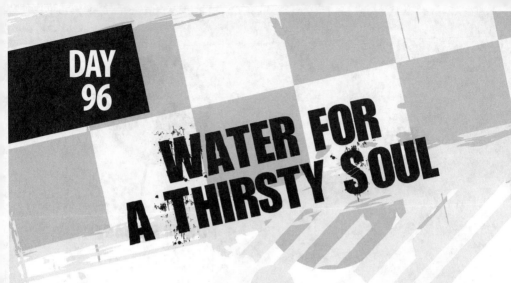

DAY 96

WATER FOR A THIRSTY SOUL

I have never been as hungry as I was during a camping trip my senior year of high school. For two days, we tried to "live off the land," which means if we weren't good fisherman, we wouldn't eat. Well, even though we were on a lake supposedly stocked with fish, I couldn't manage to get even the smallest one to bite my worm.

You'd think I could manage a day without eating a meal, but by the time we got back to the main campground, we guys were tearing into the stale doughnuts somebody left out for breakfast. Doughnuts we would have complained about on a normal day.

The Bible says that our souls are hungry. But this hunger cannot be satisfied by anything but God Himself. He created us that way.

This hunger explains why kids try alcohol or drugs. It explains why they seek pleasure in sexual relationships. They have bought the lie of the enemy that says the hunger of the soul can be filled with these things. And for a time, it seems that they satisfy. But it's like eating cotton candy. It tastes good, but soon you're reaching for the nachos or a burger.

Are you hungry today? Fill your heart and soul with the things of God. Bow before him in prayer. Drink deeply from the Word of God. Get lost in your favorite worship songs. Renew your commitment to your church and Christian friends.

Ultimately, you'll discover that nothing satisfies your soul but God. And that's just how the Creator designed you to be.

Why is it so **hard** to be **happy**?

POWER PASSAGE

As a deer pants

for flowing streams,

so pants my soul

for you, O God.

Psalm 42:1

BOTTOM LINE

Only God can satisfy the deepest longings of your heart.

OWN IT

Take some quiet time today and read the entire passage of Psalm 42.

POWER PRAYER: *Dear God, I've chased everything else and found it lacking. My soul is achingly hungry for more of You. You satisfy me as nothing else can. I want to be full of you.*

FINDING JOY IN UNEXPECTED PLACES

Weary after a long hot day on the road, Peter and the rest of the guys filed into the guest's home. As they sat down and peeled off their dusty sandals, Jesus approached with a towel over His shoulder and a basin of hot water in His hands.

Jesus, the God of the Universe, the Creator, washing my feet? I don't think so.

But it was true. The Master knelt before each of His friends and carefully scrubbed, rubbed, and soothed their aching, dirty feet.

Washing feet was the dirtiest job. That's why it was usually given to the lowest servant in the house. Nobody every volunteered. It was beneath them.

So why was Jesus washing feet? He was demonstrating to His friends and to us that humble service to others is the highest form of love.

Does that mean you should rush over to your buddies' house and offer a pedicure? Probably not. They'd think you're a bit crazy.

But Jesus's actions should motivate us to look for ways we can kneel down and serve those God has put in our lives. Maybe you could surprise your mom by helping her clean the house. Be careful, though. She might faint. Maybe you're sister is having a tough time with her homework. Could you lend her a hand? How about that elderly person across the street? Could you rake her leaves and take out her garbage?

When you follow the example of Christ by rolling up your sleeves and serving others, you'll discover that it not only helps the person you serve, it also brings you an unexpected feeling of joy.

Is there really
joy in
serving
others?

POWER PASSAGE

"If I then,

your Lord and Teacher,

have washed your feet,

you also ought to wash

one another's feet."

John 13:14

BOTTOM LINE

God calls each of us to serve others by washing their feet.

OWN IT

Ask around for someone in need at home, at church, and school. Find one physical thing you can do for them this week.

POWER PRAYER: *God, help me to have an attitude of service. Thank You for Your ultimate act of service toward me in going to the Cross. Help me to follow You by sacrificially serving others.*

DAY 98

THE POWER OF THANK YOU

Ten men came to Jesus with cracked skin, missing limbs, and rotting flesh. They suffered from one of the worst diseases known to mankind—leprosy. Lepers, in those days, were kept away from family and friends, left to disintegrate slowly to death in an isolated colony.

With one stroke, Jesus, the Great Physician granted each man a brand-new life. Now they could run, jump, work, laugh, and enjoy life again. You'd think they'd be filled with profound gratitude for Jesus's healing gift.

Only one offered thanks. The other nine left, forgetting that Jesus brought them new life. How could someone be so unthankful?

But don't we often act like the nine? We too have received healing from the hand of the Savior, spiritual healing that gives us new life and a home in heaven. Too often, we forget Jesus's gift and go our ungrateful ways.

There is power in a grateful heart. A heart that accepts each new blessing as a treasure from the Father. An undemanding heart.

Gratitude will set you apart, as it did for the one leper who communicated his joy to the Lord. Instead of joining the majority, who often complain, demand, expect, and walk away without a care, you can be the young person who always smiles and says thank you.

Today, take time for gratitude. Tell Jesus thank you for His gift of love on the Cross. Express your thanks to your parents, to your coaches, to your teachers.

You don't realize the power of thank you. Those two words just might heal a heavy heart. They might bridge a broken relationship. They might keep someone from quitting their calling.

What's the
big deal
about saying
thank you?

POWER PASSAGE

Then one of them,

when he saw that

he was healed,

turned back, praising God

with a loud voice;

and he fell on his face

at Jesus' feet,

giving him thanks.

Now he was a Samaritan.

Then Jesus answered,

"Were not ten cleansed?

Where are the nine?"

Luke 17:15–17

BOTTOM LINE

There is power in a thankful heart.

OWN IT

Sit down today and write a thank-you note to someone close to you. Take time and think about all that person has done for you. Slip the note on the person's desk or under the door. And pray God uses your words to lift that person's spirits.

POWER PRAYER: *Dear Lord, Thank You for salvation, for giving me life, and for sustaining me each day. Help me to cultivate a grateful heart.*

THE JOY OF SUFFERING

I 'll admit that James 1:2–3 presents us with a radical idea. But then again, the Bible is a radical book. Christianity is a radical religion. What is crazier than a God who Himself comes down, dies on the Cross for people who don't deserve it, and then gives them a second chance and a home in heaven forever?

So why does the Bible tell us to rejoice in trials? We have to look deeper. You see, it's all about faith. If we really believe God is in control of our lives, then we also have to believe that everything God allows is for our own good and for His glory.

Joseph could stand before the same brothers who abused, shamed, and sold him into slavery: *What you meant for evil, God meant for good* (Genesis 50:20). He could express this, because they were true in His life. The circumstances he suffered brought him to a place where God could use him to change the world. They were not the actions of a cruel God who likes to make people suffer. They were allowed by God to shape Joseph's character.

And so it is with us. Our cruel twists of fate are not random. The nasty breakup. The car accident. The divorce. If you look at them from a human perspective, each seems like one more terrible event in an unlucky life.

But what if we looked at the bad things as good things? What if we saw trials as God's hand molding our character? What if we allowed God to use our hardships to bring us to a place of powerful influence?

Then we might actually find joy in the worst possible situations. It doesn't mean we ask for trials. It doesn't mean we throw a party when

So I'm supposed to get **excited** when **bad things** happen? **Yeah, right.**

bad things happen. It doesn't mean we never cry, never get angry, never question?

It simply means we're able to smile through the pain and find joy in the most unexpected places. The dark places God allows.

BOTTOM LINE

There really can be joy in life's darkest places.

OWN IT

Check out these passages: James 1; John 15; Romans 5. What do they say about our attitude toward trials?

POWER PRAYER: *Heavenly Father, help me to identify tough times as Your touch, stretching me through trials, not intending to break me but to shape and equip me for the powerful purpose You have for my life. In Jesus's name. Amen.*

POWER PASSAGE

Count it all joy,

my brothers,

when you meet trials of

various kinds,

for you know that

the testing of your faith

produces steadfastness.

James 1:2–3

CLOSING THE BOOK

So you made it this far. Wow, I've given you a lot to chew on. Yes, I know it took you more than 100 days. Don't sweat it, you got through, and I hope God spoke to your heart each day you opened His Word.

Before I leave you, I want to drive back around to a central theme in the beginning. Maybe you've forgotten it already. Maybe you haven't.

I want to challenge you. Don't settle for the ordinary life. Don't settle for mediocre Christianity. Don't settle for something less than God created you to be.

I don't know exactly where God is going to take you. But I do know this: God wants you to be a light in a dark world, because your generation desperately needs to hear God speak through you, so others will hear the truth and come to know the same Savior you know. All around you are young people trapped by the cruel fate of sin. Will you introduce them to the God who loves them and sent His Son to die for them? You may be the only light they ever see?

Living the radical Christian life takes courage. It takes faith. It takes guts. But know that you're not alone, that the Holy Spirit who lives within you will empower you and strengthen you.

And if it counts for anything at all, know this, I believe in you. I hope our paths cross again sometime, in another book, at a conference, online, or even if you have the courage to visit my church in the Chicago area.

It's been a great ride.

How can I **live** the **radical Christian life**?

BOTTOM LINE

Don't settle for the ordinary; reach for God's best.

OWN IT

Go back through your journal pages in this book. Review your thoughts and prayers. Think about those areas where you've seen God change your heart.

POWER PRAYER: *Dear God, help me become a light in this world. Fill me with Your light so others will see it and bow their hearts in faith to You. I want to be an agent of change in my generation.*

POWER PASSAGE

"You are the light of the world. A city set on a hill cannot be hidden. "

Matthew 5:14

DELIGHT—
Finding Joy in a Hard World

Talk About It
(with your friends, your parents, or your pastor)

Daniel was ripped from his homeland and forced to live in a radically different culture. What kept Daniel and his three buddies sane through this unexpected change?

Divorce, death, and other unexpected trials can throw us for a loop. How do we make sense of life when it is turned upside down?

How can we forgive those who hurt us deeply? Is it something we can do on our own? Is it something that comes naturally?

Joseph experienced the worst kind of evil imaginable. What was it about Joseph's perspective that enabled him to process that hurt and turn it into good?

Go Deeper

Here are a few resources to help you investigate the ideas we talked about for the last 20 days.

Web sites:
crosswalk.com

biblestudytools.net

Books:
Quieting a Noisy Soul—Jim Berg

Broken: Making Sense of Life After Your Parents' Divorce—Tim Baker

No Matter What, You Can Rejoice—Michelle Glover

Movies:
Amazing Grace

New Hope® Publishers is a division of WMU®, an international organization that challenges Christian believers to understand and be radically involved in God's mission. For more information about WMU, go to www.wmu.com. More information about New Hope books may be found at www.newhopepublishers.com. New Hope books may be purchased at your local bookstore.

If you've been blessed by this book, we would like to hear your story. The publisher and author welcome your comments and suggestions at: newhopereader@wmu.org.

Other Teen Devotionals from New Hope

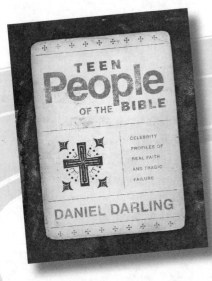

Teen People of the Bible
*Celebrity Profiles of
Real Faith and Tragic Failure*
Daniel Darling
ISBN-10: 1-59669-088-7
ISBN-13: 978-1-59669-088-2

Cherished
*Discovering the Freedom
to Love and Be Loved*
Chandra Peele
ISBN-10: 1-59669-250-2
ISBN-13: 978-1-59669-250-3

Available in bookstores
everywhere.

For information about these books or any New Hope product,
visit www.newhopepublishers.com.